AF454247

REFACTORING FOR RESILIENCE

Strengthening Systems Under Pressure

Tochukwu Njoku

DEDICATION

To the problem-solvers, the debuggers, and the relentless optimizers who see broken systems not as failures, but as puzzles waiting to be solved. And to those who taught me that resilience is not just in our code, but in our minds, our teams, and our willingness to keep learning. This book is my way of passing that lesson forward.

TABLE OF CONTENTS

FOREWORD

In today's dynamic technological landscape, system resilience is critical, given the constant pressures of scaling, potential failures, and changing user requirements. "Refactoring for Resilience: Strengthening Systems Under Pressure" offers a timely and insightful guide to constructing robust software capable of not only enduring but also thriving amidst operational challenges.

Tochukwu Njoku, leveraging a foundation of deep technical expertise and practical experience, presents an approach that extends beyond mere code refactoring. The book advocates for cultivating a resilience-oriented mindset, emphasizing the design of systems that can adapt, recover, and improve in response to disruptions.

A key strength of this work lies in its actionable guidance. Njoku provides clear strategies, well-established patterns, and pragmatic insights derived from real-world scenarios. This resource equips both seasoned architects and development professionals with the necessary tools to transform system fragility into robust strength, ensuring the creation of dependable and maintainable software.

Having observed the consequences of systems failing under stress, I recognize the significant value of the principles outlined in this book. It serves as an essential resource for anyone committed to building resilient and sustainable software solutions.

PREFACE

Software systems, much like living organisms, face constant pressure to evolve. They must handle increasing loads, resist failures, and adapt to ever-changing requirements, all while remaining maintainable. Yet, too often, we focus on short-term fixes rather than long-term resilience. This book is my attempt to change that.

Refactoring for Resilience emerged from years of wrestling with brittle systems, late-night outages, and the sobering realization that many failures could have been prevented with the right structural foundations. It's not just about writing better code; it's about designing systems that endure.

Inside, you'll find practical techniques for refactoring legacy code, patterns for fault tolerance, and strategies to future-proof your architecture. My goal is to empower you to transform chaotic, fragile systems into ones that are robust, flexible, and, above all, resilient under pressure.

A book like this is never written alone. I'm deeply grateful to the engineers, colleagues, and open-source contributors whose insights shaped these ideas. Special thanks to my reviewers and my editor for their invaluable feedback.

Whether you're refactoring a monolithic legacy system or designing a new distributed service, I hope this book becomes your trusted companion. Let's build systems that don't just survive but thrive.

INTRODUCTION

In the contemporary interconnected and rapidly changing technological landscape, systems are under unprecedented pressure from multiple directions: increasing user demands, sophisticated cyber threats, environmental challenges, and market volatility. Traditional approaches to system design that prioritize efficiency and performance under ideal conditions often crumble when confronted with unexpected stressors. This chapter establishes the fundamental principles that transform ordinary systems into resilient ones capable of withstanding, adapting, and recovering from adverse conditions.

Resilience is not merely about surviving disruption but thriving despite it. As we embark on this exploration of resilient design, we must first understand that resilience is not a feature to be added but a philosophy that must permeate every aspect of system architecture, implementation, and evolution. The foundations we establish here will serve as the bedrock upon which all subsequent resilience strategies will be built.

CHAPTER ONE

Foundations of Resilient Design

The journey toward resilient design begins with a fundamental shift in thinking. Traditional engineering emphasizes optimization under normal conditions and treats failures as exceptional cases to be handled separately. The resilience mindset inverts this approach, considering perturbations and disruptions as inevitable aspects of a system's operational reality.

This paradigm shift requires acknowledging that perfect stability is an illusion. Instead of pursuing the impossible goal of eliminating all failures, resilient design focuses on creating systems that can absorb shocks, adapt to changing conditions, and recover quickly from setbacks. This approach recognizes that the measure of a system's strength is not in how it performs under ideal circumstances but in how gracefully it handles adversity.

Adopting the resilience mindset means embracing uncertainty as a design parameter rather than an inconvenience. It means accepting that our understanding of potential threats will always be incomplete and that our systems must be prepared for anticipated and unanticipated challenges. This inherently humble perspective serves as an antidote to the hubris that often leads to catastrophic system failures.

Core Principles of Resilient Systems

Redundancy: The Power of Duplication

At its most basic level, redundancy involves having backup components or pathways that can take over when primary ones fail. However, true redundancy extends beyond simple duplication. Effective redundancy requires diversity in implementation, location, and operation to prevent common mode failures. When properly implemented, redundancy creates a system where the whole remains functional even when individual parts break down.

Redundancy takes multiple forms: physical redundancy (duplicate hardware), informational redundancy (error-correcting codes), functional redundancy (alternative methods to achieve the same outcome), and temporal redundancy (repeated attempts until success). Each form addresses different vulnerability patterns and, when strategically combined, creates layers of protection against various failure modes.

While redundancy is powerful, it comes with costs: increased complexity, potential for interference between redundant elements, and higher resource requirements. The art of resilient design includes determining the appropriate types and levels of redundancy for each system component based on its criticality and unique vulnerability profile.

Modularity: Containing Failure Propagation

Modularity divides systems into distinct components with well-defined interfaces, limiting the spread of failures across component boundaries. When one module fails, the damage is contained within that module rather than cascading throughout the entire system. This compartmentalization is essential for preventing small problems from growing into system-wide catastrophes.

Effective modularity requires more than simply breaking a system into pieces. It demands thoughtful design of module boundaries and interfaces, with careful attention to dependency management. Modules should be loosely coupled yet cohesive, allowing them to function independently while still contributing to the system's overall purpose.

Beyond its role in failure containment, modularity enhances system evolvability by allowing components to be upgraded or replaced without disrupting the entire system. This ability to evolve incrementally is itself a form of resilience, enabling systems to adapt to changing requirements and environments over time.

Adaptability and diversity expand the landscape of resilience by introducing responsiveness and variation into systems, allowing them to not just withstand disruption but actively engage with it and evolve. Where redundancy and modularity provide static strength, adaptability allows for fluid, real-time adjustments that keep a system functioning under unpredictable conditions. It's a shift from hardening systems to making them more agile, from resisting change to embracing it as part of operational continuity.

Adaptability involves an ongoing interaction between the system and its environment. An adaptable system is aware of its state and the external conditions surrounding it. This requires a robust sensing mechanism sensor in the literal sense for physical systems or monitoring software and metrics for digital ones. But sensing alone isn't enough. The system must also interpret what it senses, which demands some form of embedded intelligence, whether through rules-based logic, machine learning, or adaptive control algorithms. Then comes the real heart of adaptability: the capacity to act on that information. The system must have the structural and functional flexibility to change its behavior, reroute workflows, scale resources, or switch operating modes in response to what it perceives.

This adaptability occurs on a spectrum of timescales, each with its significance. On the short end, real-time responsiveness is crucial for immediate stability. For example, when a power grid detects an overload in one sector, it might automatically redirect flow or shed non-critical loads to prevent a wider blackout. On intermediate timescales, systems may engage in self-healing, automatically diagnosing faults and initiating repairs, like software that can restart failed services or redistribute tasks across healthy nodes. On the longest timescales, adaptability takes the form of evolution, where systems gradually restructure themselves based on long-term feedback, reconfiguring their architecture, workflows, or even core functions to meet new demands or to better withstand emerging threats.

The effectiveness of adaptation depends not only on the system's technical capabilities but also on how these capabilities are integrated. The decision-making process must be both accurate and timely. Too much delay, and the system might fail before it can adapt. Too much reactivity, and it might constantly shift in unstable or unnecessary ways. Striking the right balance is more an art than a science, requiring a nuanced understanding of context, risk, and system priorities.

Closely linked to adaptability is the concept of diversity and heterogeneity, which provide the raw material for adaptation to be meaningful. Just as ecosystems with varied species tend to recover more effectively from shocks, technical systems with diverse components are better able to withstand unexpected disruptions. Homogeneity is efficient, but it comes with a hidden cost: a single flaw or vulnerability can cascade across all identical units. This is especially dangerous in systems that rely on large-scale replication, such as fleets of devices running the same firmware or cloud systems built on uniform architectures.

Introducing diversity can take many forms. It might mean using different vendors for critical hardware components, deploying software on a mix of operating systems, or implementing key functions using multiple approaches say, one deterministic and one probabilistic. Even at the organizational level, operational diversity matters: different teams applying varied practices or perspectives can spot problems that uniform groups might overlook. These layers of variation create fault-tolerant ecosystems where the failure of one element doesn't predict the failure of others.

But diversity isn't free. It increases the complexity of integration and management. Systems built from varied parts are harder to standardize, test, and optimize. They require broader expertise from their maintainers and more sophisticated orchestration to ensure that all the different components can still work together. Without careful governance, diversity can devolve into fragmentation, where components become incompatible or unmanageable. The goal, then, is not diversity for its own sake, but strategic diversity variation introduced where it offers the most protection against specific risks.

Ultimately, adaptability and diversity form the foundation of systems that are not just robust but truly resilient in the deepest sense. They don't just resist disruption, they engage with it, respond to it, and often come out stronger. They recognize that change is not an anomaly but a constant, and they are built not just to survive it but to grow through it. In this light, resilience becomes not a fixed trait but a living capacity, cultivated through feedback, variation, and the ongoing dance between order and change.

Margin and Overprovisioning

Resilient systems are fundamentally about more than just surviving failures. They are about absorbing, adapting, and continuing to operate in meaningful ways under strain. One of the subtle but vital design choices that enables this is the deliberate inclusion of margin. Margin is not just about having extra; it is a calculated buffer that allows systems to remain stable in the face of variability, spikes in demand, partial degradation, or unanticipated stressors. It is a form of preparedness that buys time, space, and flexibility when things do not go according to plan, which they almost inevitably won't.

The concept of margin becomes most apparent when a system is pushed beyond its typical load. A server designed to run at 80% capacity may function flawlessly under normal conditions, but if no margin is built in, a sudden burst of traffic could push it over the edge, resulting in cascading failures. With a margin, the same server might operate well under 50%, absorbing bursts without breaking down. The same applies in project timelines, where buffer periods absorb delays without derailing delivery. In power grids, battery reserves can carry critical loads during an outage. In networks, bandwidth headroom can accommodate congestion or rerouting. Across all these domains, margin plays a protective, stabilizing role.

But designing with margin is as much an art as it is a science. Excessive margin can lead to resource underutilization and wasted investment, which can be especially problematic in environments with tight budgets or limited infrastructure. On the other hand, inadequate margin creates fragility, where even minor deviations from expected conditions can push the system into failure. The key is calibration: understanding historical data, modeling potential stress scenarios, and evaluating trade-offs between efficiency and resilience. It also means revisiting margin levels periodically, since what constitutes sufficient headroom can change over time as workloads evolve and systems scale.

Closely related to margin is the principle of graceful degradation. Resilience is not only about withstanding load or avoiding collapse; it's about managing failure in ways that preserve functionality and user trust. In real-world systems, total failure is rare when graceful degradation is built in. Instead of going dark, the system adapts, dropping non-critical services, switching to basic modes, or slowing down fewer essential processes to preserve the core. For users, this often manifests as reduced functionality or quality rather than a complete outage, which is far more tolerable and recoverable.

Graceful degradation relies on clarity about what matters most. In a communications platform, maintaining text messages might take precedence over video calls. In an e-commerce site, showing cached pages and accepting payments might be prioritized, even if recommendations or real-time inventory updates fail. This prioritization requires foresight and deep understanding of user needs, business objectives, and system interdependencies. It must be encoded into the system's behavior, ideally through automated detection of stress and well-defined fallback modes that are tested as rigorously as the primary functions.

The ability to degrade without disintegration also hinges on architectural choices like loose coupling. Systems composed of tightly interdependent components are prone to failure propagation, when one part fails, it pulls others down with it. But in loosely coupled systems, boundaries are respected, and components can operate in isolation or limited modes if necessary. This separation allows for targeted degradation and local recovery, enabling systems to remain partially operational even as they absorb or respond to faults.

What's essential to recognize is that neither margin nor graceful degradation can be tacked on at the end of development. They require early and deliberate thinking. These characteristics emerge from choices made in how systems are structured, how dependencies are managed, how priorities are defined, and how variability is anticipated. The benefits, however, are profound. Systems built with margin and capable of graceful degradation inspire confidence because they are visibly prepared for the unexpected. They embody a calm under pressure, not by resisting disruption blindly, but by adapting intelligently and prioritizing what matters most. In a world where change and failure are constants, this kind of design is not a luxury; it's a necessity.

Designing for Recovery

Even the most resilient systems will occasionally fail. Truly resilient design acknowledges this reality and incorporates mechanisms for rapid recovery. These include state preservation capabilities that maintain critical information during failures, restart protocols that bring systems back online in a controlled manner, and reconciliation processes that restore consistency after disruptions.

Recovery design considers not just technical mechanisms but also human factors. Clear procedures, intuitive diagnostics, and effective tools enable operators to quickly identify and address problems. Training and simulation prepare teams to respond effectively even under the stress of actual emergencies.

The speed and completeness of recovery often determine the ultimate impact of a failure event. By designing systems with recovery in mind, we transform potentially catastrophic incidents into manageable disruptions with limited consequences.

The Resilience Trade-Off Matrix

Resilience does not come without costs. Each resilience-enhancing strategy introduces its demands in terms of resources, complexity, or performance overhead. The resilience trade-off matrix provides a framework for evaluating these costs against the protective benefits they provide.

This matrix considers factors including

- Implementation cost versus protection value

- Performance impact versus failure mitigation capability

- Complexity increases versus resilience gain

- Maintenance burden versus recovery enhancement

By explicitly mapping these trade-offs, designers can make informed decisions about where and how to invest in resilience. This analytical approach ensures that resilience features deliver maximum value while minimizing negative impacts on other system qualities.

Measuring and Benchmarking Resilience

You cannot improve what you cannot measure. Establishing metrics and benchmarks for resilience is essential for both initial design validation and ongoing system improvement. These measurements must go beyond simple availability percentages to capture the multidimensional nature of resilience.

Comprehensive resilience metrics include:

- Recovery time objectives (RTO) and recovery point objectives (RPO)

- Degradation profiles under various stress scenarios

- Adaptation speed in response to changing conditions

- Failure containment effectiveness

- System survival thresholds for different stress types

These metrics should be regularly tested through controlled experiments, simulations, and game days where failure modes are deliberately triggered to evaluate system response. Such testing not only validates design decisions but also builds organizational muscle memory for responding to real incidents.

Resilience as Foundational Philosophy

Resilience, when properly understood, transcends the idea of a technical fix or a checklist item. It is not something that can be patched on after a system is built, nor is it confined to isolated components or one-off projects. Instead, it must be a guiding philosophy and ethos that shapes every decision, from early design choices to long-term maintenance and organizational culture. The most enduring systems are those in which resilience is treated as a first-class concern, embedded not just in the architecture but in the mindset of the teams that build and sustain them.

Integrating resilience into the core of system design means approaching every component, interface, and dependency with an awareness of failure as a natural, even expected, part of the system's lifecycle. It involves asking hard questions from the outset: What happens when this component fails? How will the system behave under stress? Are we prepared for the unexpected? This proactive orientation requires humility a recognition that no matter how confident we are in our design or assumptions, real-world conditions will always introduce uncertainty, complexity, and disruption.

As the journey continues through the practical dimensions of building resilient systems, the abstract principles begin to crystallize into concrete techniques. Patterns for refactoring monoliths into services, strategies for decoupling tightly bound components, practices for monitoring, chaos engineering, load balancing, and graceful degradation, all of these become expressions of the deeper principles of redundancy, modularity, adaptability, and diversity. They are not standalone tools but manifestations of a coherent worldview that prioritizes resilience as essential, not optional.

Yet applying these principles is not a one-time act. The process of building resilient systems is iterative, ongoing, and deeply human. It requires vigilance and openness to feedback, both from systems themselves and from the people who interact with them. It involves learning from failure, not just fixing it, but understanding it deeply, tracing its roots, and redesigning processes or structures so that similar breakdowns are less likely to recur. This continuous learning loop transforms isolated incidents into institutional knowledge and temporary fixes into lasting improvements.

Organizational alignment is equally important. Resilience at the technical level must be mirrored by resilience at the cultural and structural levels. Teams must be empowered to prioritize long-term stability over short-term speed, to invest in preventive maintenance, to question brittle conventions, and to advocate for changes that improve robustness even when the benefits are not immediately visible. Leadership plays a vital role in setting the tone, allocating the time and resources needed for resilient practices, and encouraging a culture of experimentation and psychological safety.

In this broader view, the pursuit of resilience becomes a kind of systems wisdom a philosophy of design and operation rooted in realism, adaptability, and care. It accepts that failure is inevitable but insists that failure need not be catastrophic. It acknowledges complexity but doesn't shy away from managing it. It recognizes the interdependence of systems and people and strives to build structures where that interdependence becomes a source of strength, not vulnerability.

By fully committing to the principles discussed, organizations position themselves not only to survive disruption but to evolve through it. They create systems that are not frozen in time but capable of growth and transformation. The road to resilience, then, is not about reaching a perfect ending state but about fostering a continuous, adaptive, and forward-looking posture, one where every challenge becomes an opportunity to learn, strengthen, and renew.

CHAPTER TWO

Pressure Points Identifying System Vulnerabilities

Understanding where and how systems break down under pressure is the essential first step toward building true resilience. This chapter explores the methodical identification of vulnerability points, those critical junctures where pressure concentrates and failures originate. Just as a physician must diagnose before prescribing treatment, engineers and architects must identify vulnerabilities before implementing effective resilience measures.

System vulnerabilities rarely announce themselves before failure occurs. They hide within complex interactions, emerge from seemingly innocuous design decisions, and often remain invisible until triggered by specific combinations of circumstances. By developing a systematic approach to vulnerability identification, we transform this invisible landscape of risk into a visible map that guides our resilience efforts. The goal is not to eliminate all vulnerabilities an impossible task in any complex system but rather to understand them deeply enough to implement appropriate countermeasures. As we'll discover, some vulnerabilities require reinforcement, others demand redesign, and still others are best addressed through monitoring and rapid response capabilities. The art of resilient design lies in matching the right remediation strategy to each vulnerability's unique characteristics.

The Vulnerability Spectrum

System vulnerabilities span a wide spectrum, from readily apparent structural weaknesses to subtle emergent behaviors that manifest only under specific conditions. Understanding this spectrum helps us develop comprehensive identification strategies that leave no blind spots in our analysis.

At one end of the spectrum are direct vulnerabilities straightforward weaknesses in system components or connections. These include physical limitations (processing capacity, bandwidth constraints), design flaws (inadequate error handling, poor exception management), and implementation defects (memory leaks, race conditions). Such vulnerabilities typically manifest as isolated failures in specific components or functions. At the opposite end are emergent vulnerabilities that arise from the interaction of multiple components, each potentially robust in isolation. These include cascading failures, resource contention scenarios, deadlock conditions, and performance degradation under specific workload patterns. Such vulnerabilities often remain hidden during component-level testing and emerge only when the integrated system operates under real-world conditions.

Between these extremes lies a continuum of vulnerabilities with varying degrees of complexity and visibility. By recognizing this spectrum, we can develop identification strategies that encompass the full range of potential failure modes, from the obvious to the obscure.

Dependency Mapping and Critical Path Analysis

Every system comprises a web of dependencies, components that rely on each other to function properly. These dependencies create natural vulnerability points where failures can propagate through the system. Identifying and mapping these dependencies is therefore fundamental to understanding system vulnerabilities. Dependency mapping begins with documenting the explicit dependencies designed into the system: service calls, data flows, shared resources, and operational sequences. These relationships form the skeleton of our vulnerability map, highlighting the pathways through which failures can potentially spread.

However, explicit dependencies tell only part of the story. Equally important are implicit dependencies, unstated assumptions about timing, resource availability, data formats, or environmental conditions. These invisible dependencies often harbor the most insidious vulnerabilities, as they operate outside our formal models and expectations.

Once dependencies are mapped, critical path analysis identifies the sequences of operations with zero slack, those where any delay or failure directly impacts overall system performance or availability. These critical paths represent natural pressure points where even minor disruptions can have outsized consequences. By identifying these paths, we can prioritize resilience investments where they deliver maximum value. The most sophisticated dependency mapping incorporates not just technical dependencies but also organizational ones. Systems often rely on specific teams, knowledge holders, or decision processes. When these human elements form part of critical paths, they introduce their vulnerability patterns that must be recognized and addressed.

Load and Stress Testing: Revealing Hidden Breaking Points

Theoretical analysis can identify many vulnerabilities, but some reveal themselves only under actual stress. Comprehensive testing regimes that deliberately push systems beyond their expected operating parameters are essential for uncovering these hidden breaking points. Load testing applies gradually increasing pressure to the system, measuring how performance degrades as demand approaches and exceeds the designed capacity. These tests reveal bottlenecks, resource limitations, and scalability constraints that might otherwise remain hidden until encountered in production.

Stress testing takes this concept further, subjecting the system to extreme, often unrealistic conditions to identify ultimate breaking points. By pushing components to failure in controlled environments, we learn not just where systems break but how they break knowledge critical for designing appropriate resilience mechanisms.

Chaos engineering extends these approaches by introducing random or targeted disruptions into production or production-like environments. By deliberately creating failures terminating services, introducing latency, corrupting data, and conducting chaos experiments reveals how the system responds to realistic failure scenarios. These techniques have evolved from simple "chaos monkeys" to sophisticated platforms for hypothesis-driven resilience testing. The most effective testing regimes combine multiple approaches, varying not just the magnitude of stress but also its nature, duration, and pattern. Systems that withstand constant high loads may collapse under bursty traffic; components resilient to hardware failures may falter when faced with network partitions. Only by exploring this full-dimensional space of potential stressors can we build a comprehensive vulnerability map.

Failure Mode and Effects Analysis is more than just a checklist activity it's a disciplined mindset that forces teams to confront the full spectrum of potential breakdowns in a system. While it has its roots in hardware engineering, where physical tolerances and failure thresholds are more predictable, its core principles translate seamlessly into the digital world. In software and complex hybrid systems, where dependencies can be abstract and behaviors emergent, FMEA serves as a crucial anchor. It helps teams' step back from their assumptions and interrogate the system piece by piece, not to predict failure with perfect accuracy, but to reveal blind spots and reduce the probability of being caught off guard.

At its most basic level, the FMEA process compels a granular dissection of a system looking at every module, every interaction point, and every function to ask what might go wrong. This disciplined repetition of asking how, why, and what next creates space for non-obvious insights to surface. It forces a shift from reactive thinking to anticipatory design, helping teams think not just about how the system is supposed to work, but how it might fail, especially under stress or in edge cases that rarely show up in standard testing. This focus on failure as a starting point challenges the optimism bias that often clouds system design, especially in early stages when teams are focused on features and delivery.

The real strength of FMEA begins to show when it moves from qualitative speculation to quantitative assessment. Assigning severity, likelihood, and detectability scores transforms the conversation from general concern to targeted action. It gives structure to the chaos of risk by making it measurable. The Risk Priority Number, while not a perfect metric, serves as a rough but powerful guide to resource allocation. It helps avoid the trap of focusing on the most obvious or recent failure and instead directs attention to the combinations of severity and frequency that represent the greatest systemic threat. This data-driven prioritization is especially vital in environments where time, people, and budgets are limited where every mitigation effort carries an opportunity cost.

But FMEA becomes even more insightful when it expands beyond isolated components. Most real-world failures don't originate from a single part breaking they emerge at the seams. Interfaces, where components pass control or data between each other, are often the least well-understood and most vulnerable parts of a system. Different teams may own different parts, documentation may be incomplete, and assumptions may silently diverge. These boundary conditions are fertile ground for failure modes that don't show up in unit tests but manifest only when systems interact under load or under stress. FMEA that actively targets these interface zones can surface the kinds of latent vulnerabilities that are most likely to be missed by conventional design reviews.

Even more valuable is the application of FMEA at the system level, where cascading effects and compound failures come into focus. A single component failure might be harmless on its own but, when paired with a delay in detection and a failure in a redundant backup, could trigger a chain reaction. FMEA encourages exploration of these layered scenarios where multiple small issues align to produce a major outage. Thinking in terms of these compounded risks helps prevent underestimating vulnerabilities that might appear minor in isolation but are dangerous in combination.

The iterative nature of FMEA is just as important as its initial rigor. Systems don't remain static. Code changes, workloads shift, usage patterns evolve, and new integrations emerge. If FMEA is only conducted at the beginning of a project or in response to a failure, it becomes stale and eventually irrelevant. To be effective, it must be embedded as a living part of the system lifecycle, reviewed regularly, and revisited whenever significant changes are made. This continuity allows for the refinement of risk models, the updating of assumptions, and the integration of lessons learned from real-world incidents.

Furthermore, when teams across disciplines engage in the FMEA process developers, operations, product managers, security specialists the process becomes a powerful alignment tool. It facilitates a shared understanding of system behavior, interdependencies, and critical vulnerabilities. It cultivates a culture of collective ownership over resilience, rather than distributing responsibility unevenly or assuming that someone else will handle it. The shared language of risk, supported by the structured methodology of FMEA, helps bridge the communication gaps that often exist in complex systems.

In this way, FMEA becomes more than a technique, it becomes a strategic practice. It blends structured analysis with human insight, helping teams stay grounded in reality while navigating complexity. Its value lies not just in identifying what might go wrong, but in shifting how organizations think about risk, responsibility, and the nature of robust systems. Over time, this kind of thinking pays dividends not only in preventing failure, but in building systems that are prepared to endure, adapt, and thrive in the face of inevitable uncertainty.

Weakest Link Analysis: Finding the Breaking Point

Complex systems rarely fail uniformly across all components. Instead, they break at their weakest points, the components, connections, or processes with the lowest tolerance for pressure. Identifying these weakest links provides natural starting points for resilience improvements.

Weakest link analysis examines each system element through multiple lenses: capacity limits, failure rates, error handling capabilities, recovery mechanisms, and degradation patterns. It asks not just "Where is this component vulnerable?" but also "How much pressure can this component withstand before failure?" and "What happens when this component fails?" This analysis must consider not just technical elements but also organizational and process factors that influence system resilience. Teams with key knowledge silos, processes with manual choke points, or operations dependent on specific individuals often constitute organizational weak links that undermine otherwise robust technical architectures. The most sophisticated weak link analyses incorporate quantitative models that simulate how different pressure levels affect each component. These models help identify not just the current weakest link but also the next-weakest link that will become the limiting factor once the first is strengthened, vital knowledge for planning comprehensive resilience improvements.

Threat Modeling and Attack Surface Analysis

Not all vulnerabilities arise from accidents or random events; many results from deliberate attacks by adversaries seeking to exploit system weaknesses. Threat modeling identifies these intentional threat vectors, and the attack surfaces they target, adding another critical dimension to our vulnerability map.

Effective threat modeling begins by identifying potential adversaries and their motivations: criminal actors seeking financial gain, competitors pursuing business advantage, nation-states conducting espionage, or insiders with malicious intent. Each adversary class brings different capabilities, techniques, and objectives that shape the threats they pose. With adversaries defined, analysis shifts to attack surfaces the sum of all points where an unauthorized user could enter or extract data from the system. These include network interfaces, API endpoints, user interfaces, data storage systems, and physical access points. Each attack surface presents unique vulnerability patterns that must be identified and addressed.

The STRIDE framework (spoofing, tampering, repudiation, information disclosure, denial of service, and elevation of privilege) provides a structured approach for analyzing potential threats against each attack surface. By systematically exploring how each threat type might manifest, teams build a comprehensive catalog of security vulnerabilities. Security vulnerabilities often interact with other system weaknesses in complex ways. An otherwise minor performance bottleneck becomes critical when exploited in a denial-of-service attack; a small data validation oversight becomes catastrophic when leveraged for privilege escalation. Understanding these interactions is essential for comprehensive vulnerability assessment.

Latent Failure Analysis: The Hidden Time Bombs

Latent failures are the silent threats within systems, quietly accumulating risk while giving the illusion of normalcy. Unlike overt failures that trigger immediate alarms, these vulnerabilities lie beneath the surface, undetected and often misunderstood, waiting for the right, or wrong, combination of factors to emerge. What makes them particularly dangerous is not just their invisibility but their ability to remain dormant for extended periods, sometimes years, before causing a sudden and severe disruption. By the time they surface, the damage is often deep and wide, precisely because no one saw it coming.

These failures are typically embedded in the system's fabric flaws in logic that only appear under rare input combinations, configuration mismatches that result from cumulative updates, or gradual performance degradations that are so subtle they pass unnoticed in daily operations. They can be the consequence of well-meaning but incomplete fixes, shortcuts taken during delivery pressure, or even long-forgotten decisions made during initial design. Over time, as the environment changes and systems evolve, these dormant flaws inch closer to activation, often catalyzed by an unusual traffic pattern, a coincidental failure elsewhere, or a manual intervention that tips the balance.

Detecting these threats is a different challenge altogether. Because they're not breaking anything yet, conventional monitoring and alerting systems typically don't flag them. Instead, a more forensic and proactive approach is required, combining a deep understanding of both the system's behavior and its structure. Static code analysis, for example, can uncover unreachable logic paths, unsafe memory usage, or unhandled edge cases that would otherwise go unnoticed. Runtime instrumentation can surface low-frequency anomalies or unusual sequences of operations that may signal a slow-building problem. But even these tools must be paired with context-aware interpretation; knowing what to look for and how to prioritize findings is half the battle.

Trend analysis can also be a powerful tool when tuned correctly. A memory leak that slowly consumes resources may be imperceptible in early stages, but with the right historical lens, the pattern becomes clear. Similarly, tracking response time variations, error rates under specific loads, or usage spikes tied to feature deployments can reveal early signs of emerging instability. These clues require not just tools but habits: a culture of curiosity, disciplined data collection, and the willingness to question what appears to be working.

Configuration drift is another frequent source of latent failure. Systems are rarely static, and over time, small changes, whether automated, manual, or uncoordinated can accumulate into a misalignment between the intended and actual state. A permissions setting altered for one purpose may inadvertently expose a vulnerability months later. A dependency updated in one part of the system but not another might lead to subtle inconsistencies or incompatibilities that remain dormant until a specific condition forces their interaction. Configuration auditing systematically comparing the current state against approved baselines, becomes essential in surfacing these hidden divergences before they become disruptive.

Perhaps the most difficult to quantify, yet equally critical, is the accumulation of technical debt. When systems are rushed into production or patched repeatedly without a broader redesign, they accrue compromises that make them more brittle over time. These debts, like financial ones, carry interest: every workaround and deferred fix increases future maintenance costs and reduces the margin for adaptation. Left unchecked, they manifest as rigid systems that resist change and fail under pressure, not because of a single fault, but because they can no longer absorb or adapt to the unexpected.

A particularly dangerous dimension of latent failure lies in system boundaries. These are the transition zones between services, teams, or stages in a workflow. At these junctions, assumptions are often made but rarely verified about what data will be passed, how errors will be handled, or who is responsible for what. Since these areas tend to fall between the responsibilities of individual teams or components, they are also zones of reduced visibility. Misaligned interfaces, incompatible expectations, or uncoordinated updates can create vulnerabilities that neither side fully understands until something breaks.

Addressing latent failures requires more than just tools; it demands organizational commitment. It means allocating time for preventive work, encouraging cross-team visibility, maintaining architectural hygiene, and fostering a mindset that prioritizes long-term health over short-term deliverables. It calls for a culture where anomalies are investigated rather than ignored, where minor glitches are not brushed aside because "it still works," and where people are empowered to ask, "What could go wrong?" even when everything appears stable. In this way, resilience is not only built into the system; it's embedded into the practice of building itself.

Impact Analysis and Fault Trees

Understanding how vulnerabilities cascade through a system is essential for accurate risk assessment. Impact analysis and fault tree methods provide formal techniques for mapping these propagation patterns and identifying the compound vulnerabilities they create.

Impact analysis begins with a potential failure and traces its effects forward through the system, documenting how the initial failure propagates, transforms, and potentially amplifies as it affects dependent components. This forward-looking analysis reveals vulnerability chains where minor initial failures can grow into major system disruptions. Fault tree analysis works in the reverse direction, starting with a potential system-level failure and working backward to identify all possible chains of events that could cause it. This approach creates a logical tree of failure preconditions, helping teams identify vulnerability combinations that might be missed when examining components in isolation.

These techniques are particularly valuable for identifying non-obvious vulnerability patterns, such as Common cause failures, where a single event simultaneously affects multiple components Hidden coupling, where supposedly independent components fail together due to shared dependencies Failure masking, where one component's failure hides another's, complicating diagnosis and repair Recovery interference, where the failure of one component prevents others from executing their recovery procedures. By mapping these complex interaction patterns, teams gain a more sophisticated understanding of system vulnerabilities that goes beyond simple component-level analysis.

The Human Element: Cognitive and Organizational Vulnerabilities

Technical systems do not exist in isolation; they operate within human and organizational contexts that introduce their vulnerability patterns. A comprehensive vulnerability assessment must consider these human factors alongside technical ones.

Cognitive vulnerabilities arise from predictable patterns in human decision-making and perception. These include confirmation bias, where operators see what they expect to see rather than what's happening automation complacency, where monitoring effectiveness degrades as systems run smoothly for extended periods Alert fatigue, where numerous warnings cause important signals to be missed or ignored; Overconfidence in models and projections that don't reflect real-world complexity.

Organizational vulnerabilities stem from structures, processes, and cultures that undermine system resilience. Common examples include; knowledge silos, where critical information is concentrated in specific individuals or teams' coordination breakdowns between groups with shared responsibility for system components misaligned incentives that prioritize features or deadlines over reliability and security and cultural aversions to sharing bad news or reporting emerging problems.

These human and organizational vulnerabilities often interact with technical ones in dangerous ways. A minor technical issue becomes catastrophic when combined with operator fatigue; a recoverable failure turns permanent when organizational silos prevent effective response coordination. Identifying these human factors requires different techniques from technical vulnerability assessment. Observational studies, procedure reviews, near-miss analyses, and cultural surveys all provide valuable insights into how human and organizational factors contribute to system vulnerability.

Translating Vulnerabilities into Action: The Remediation Roadmap

Identifying vulnerabilities creates no value unless it leads to action. The final section of this chapter focuses on transforming vulnerability insights into practical remediation strategies prioritized for maximum resilience impact.

Not all vulnerabilities require immediate fixes. Some are best addressed through monitoring and detection, others through containment strategies, and still others through acceptance and contingency planning. The remediation roadmap must match each vulnerability with the most appropriate response strategy based on:

Risk level, combining impact severity and occurrence probability. Remediation cost and complexity, including both implementation and ongoing maintenance, and time to implement effective countermeasures. Dependencies between vulnerabilities and their remediation

Prioritization frameworks help teams allocate limited resilience resources for maximum effect. These frameworks typically balance multiple factors, including.

Critical path vulnerabilities that directly impact essential system functions, Common mode vulnerabilities that could simultaneously affect multiple components, Vulnerabilities with minimal detection or warning time, Vulnerabilities exploitable by identified adversaries and vulnerabilities in components with long repair or recovery times.

The resulting remediation roadmap should span multiple time horizons: immediate actions to address urgent vulnerabilities, medium-term projects to strengthen key pressure points, and longer-term architectural evolution to eliminate structural weaknesses. This time-based approach ensures both rapid risk reduction and sustainable resilience improvement.

This chapter has explored techniques for identifying system vulnerabilities across the full spectrum of potential failure modes. By systematically mapping dependencies, testing boundaries, analyzing failure propagation, and considering human factors, we transform vague concerns about system fragility into concrete vulnerability inventories that guide resilience investments.

The vulnerability map we've created serves as the foundation for all subsequent resilience work. It tells us where to focus redundancy efforts, which interfaces need redesign, where monitoring must be enhanced, and which recovery mechanisms require strengthening. Without this map, resilience initiatives become unfocused and inefficient, potentially missing critical vulnerabilities while overinvesting in already-robust areas. As we move forward to subsequent chapters on specific resilience techniques and architectural patterns, we'll repeatedly reference this vulnerability mapping process. Each resilience strategy we explore will address specific vulnerability patterns identified through the techniques covered here. The most effective resilience programs maintain a continuous dialogue between vulnerability identification and resilience implementation, with each informing and refining the other.

Remember that vulnerability mapping is not a one-time exercise but an ongoing process that must evolve as systems change, new threats emerge, and our understanding deepens. The most resilient organizations institutionalize vulnerability identification, making it a continuous aspect of system development and operation rather than an occasional special project.

CHAPTER THREE

The Graceful Failure Paradigm

Introduction: Embracing Inevitable Failure

Perfect reliability is an unattainable ideal in complex systems. Despite our best efforts at prevention, failures will occur, whether from unforeseen circumstances, extreme loads, external dependencies, or simply the probabilistic nature of component behavior at scale. The graceful failure paradigm represents a fundamental shift in how we approach system resilience: instead of futilely pursuing perfect reliability, we design systems that maintain core functionality and preserve user experience even as components fail.

This perspective transforms how we think about failure. Rather than viewing it as an exceptional condition to be avoided at all costs, we recognize failure as an inherent aspect of system operation to be managed and contained. The question becomes not if our systems will experience failure, but how they will behave when they do. Graceful failure means systems degrade predictably rather than collapse catastrophically, maintaining essential services even as secondary functions become compromised.

The Failure Spectrum: Beyond Binary Thinking

Traditional system design often treats failure as a binary condition; systems are either functioning correctly or they're not. This oversimplification leads to brittle architectures that work perfectly until they suddenly don't. The graceful failure paradigm begins by recognizing that failure exists on a spectrum, with many possible states between "fully operational" and "completely non-functional".

At one end of this spectrum is perfect operation, where all system components function as designed and all services meet their full specifications. At the other end is complete failure, where the system provides no functionality whatsoever. Between these extremes lie various degraded states where some components or functions operate normally while others are compromised or unavailable.

Understanding this spectrum is essential for designing graceful degradation paths. It enables us to map the possible system states under different failure conditions and identify acceptable degraded modes that preserve essential functionality. This mapping process starts by asking, what is the minimum viable service our system must maintain under extreme conditions? What functions can be temporarily sacrificed to preserve core capabilities? How should service quality degrade as resources become constrained?

By answering these questions, we develop a failure model that guides architectural decisions, implementation priorities, and operational responses. This model transforms vague aspirations for "robustness" into concrete specifications for how the system should behave under specific failure scenarios.

Critical Function Preservation: Defining What Must Work

Not all system functions are equally important. Some represent core capabilities essential to the system's purpose, while others provide enhancements or conveniences that, while valuable, aren't fundamental to the system's mission. Identifying and preserving these critical functions is the central tenet of the graceful failure paradigm.

The process begins with function categorization, explicitly classifying each system capability according to its importance. Common categorization schemes include

These are the essential capabilities without which the system cannot fulfill its primary purpose. For an e-commerce platform, processing payments is mission-critical; for a medical monitoring system, transmitting vital signs is mission-critical; for a communications platform, delivering messages is mission-critical. These functions must be preserved even under the most extreme failure conditions. These functions, while not defining the system's core purpose, are nonetheless essential for organizational operations. They may include reporting capabilities, administrative interfaces, or integration with other business systems. Business-critical functions should be preserved whenever possible but can be temporarily compromised to maintain mission-critical capabilities if necessary. These enhance the user experience but aren't essential to either the system's primary purpose or business operations. They include convenience features, advanced visualizations, or optional integrations. Value-added functions are the first to be sacrificed when the system is under pressure. This categorization isn't merely an academic exercise, it directly informs architectural decisions, resource allocation, and failure response strategies. Mission-critical functions receive the highest levels of redundancy, the most robust implementation, and priority access to resources during degraded operation. Value-added functions, in contrast, are designed to be cleanly disabled, when necessary, without affecting core system behavior.

The most sophisticated implementations go beyond static categorization to implement dynamic criticality assessments that consider context, timing, and user needs. A function might be value-added for most users but mission-critical for specific user segments; a capability might be business-critical during business hours but less important during off-hours. These nuanced models enable more precise degradation strategies that maximize preserved value under varying conditions.

Failure Isolation: Containing the Damage

When components inevitably fail, the difference between graceful degradation and catastrophic collapse often comes down to failure isolation the ability to contain problems within well-defined boundaries rather than allowing them to propagate throughout the system. Effective isolation mechanisms limit the blast radius of failures, enabling the remaining components to continue functioning despite localized problems.

Inspired by naval architecture, where ships are divided into watertight compartments to prevent flooding from sinking the entire vessel, the bulkhead pattern divides systems into isolated compartments that can fail independently. Each compartment contains specific functionality with controlled interfaces to other compartments, preventing failures from spreading beyond their boundaries. Implementing bulkheads requires thoughtful system decomposition, with careful attention to both logical and physical isolation. At the logical level, this means a clean separation of concerns with well-defined interfaces between components. At the physical level, it may involve dedicated infrastructure, separate process spaces, or distinct deployment units for each compartment. Modern containerization and microservice architectures inherently support bulkhead implementation by packaging functionality into discrete, independently deployable units. However, true isolation requires more than just deployment separation, it demands careful management of shared resources, communication patterns, and failure propagation paths.

Circuit Breakers and Failure Detection

Fast failure detection and response are essential for effective isolation. Circuit breakers, components that monitor failures and automatically stop operation when problems are detected, serve as the nervous system of gracefully failing architectures. They prevent cascading failures by quickly isolating problematic components before they can affect the broader system. The basic circuit breaker pattern is simple: monitor for failures in a component or dependency, and when failures exceed a threshold, "trip" the circuit to prevent further calls to the failing component. Once tripped, the circuit breaker periodically tests the component to determine if it has recovered, automatically resuming normal operation when appropriate. Advanced circuit breakers incorporate sophisticated failure detection mechanisms, adaptive thresholds that adjust based on observed patterns, and partial tripping strategies that allow some traffic through even in degraded states. They may also implement fallback mechanisms that provide alternative functionality when primary components fail.

Designing Degradation Paths: The Art of Failing Less

When systems encounter conditions beyond their design parameters, they must transition from full functionality to various degraded states in ways that preserve maximum value. Designing these degradation paths, the sequences of functionality reductions a system follows under increasing pressure, is a critical aspect of the graceful failure paradigm.

Perhaps the simplest degradation strategy is progressive feature reduction selectively disabling non-essential functions to preserve resources for critical capabilities. This approach requires not just identifying which features to disable first (based on the criticality categories discussed earlier) but also designing components so they can be cleanly disabled without disrupting the remaining system.

Effective feature reduction mechanisms include feature flags that can dynamically enable or disable capabilities, configuration systems that support runtime adjustments to service levels, and load shedding algorithms that selectively reject lower-priority work during overload conditions.

The most sophisticated implementations apply progressive reduction differently across user segments, preserving full functionality for critical users while reducing features for others. This differentiated degradation maximizes overall business value by protecting the most important transactions even as the system scales back services for less critical interactions.

Quality of Service Tiering

Rather than completely disabling features, quality of service tiering reduces the resources allocated to non-critical functions while maintaining their basic availability. This approach preserves the breadth of functionality at the expense of performance or completeness in non-essential areas.

Common quality tiering strategies include

Reducing result completeness (returning partial or summarized data) Increasing response latency for lower-priority functions Lowering refresh rates or update frequencies for non-critical information Decreasing resolution or fidelity for resource-intensive outputs Simplifying algorithms or processing logic during high-load conditions. These adjustments allow systems to gracefully stretch limited resources across all functions rather than maintaining full quality for some capabilities while completely eliminating others.

Degradation paths can be either statically defined or dynamically determined based on runtime conditions. Static degradation follows predefined paths established during system design; specific features are disabled in a predetermined sequence as conditions deteriorate. This approach provides predictability but may lack flexibility in responding to novel failure scenarios.

Dynamic degradation, in contrast, uses runtime information about system conditions, user needs, and business priorities to determine optimal service reductions. This approach requires more sophisticated monitoring and decision-making mechanisms but can preserve more value by adapting degradation strategies to specific circumstances. The most effective systems combine both approaches, with predefined degradation paths that capture known best practices while allowing for dynamic adjustments based on actual conditions. This hybrid model provides stability through well-understood behaviors while maintaining adaptability to unexpected situations.

Failure Transparency: Communicating Degraded States

Failure transparency sits at the intersection of technical resilience and human experience. It's not just about how systems respond to failure internally but how they present that reality to those interacting with them, both users and operators. In many ways, the perception of a system's reliability is shaped less by the absence of failure and more by how well failure is handled when it occurs. When systems are silent in the face of degradation, or worse, misrepresent their state as healthy, they not only frustrate users but also erode trust. On the other hand, when a system clearly and calmly communicates its current limitations and what users can expect, it transforms a negative experience into one that feels respectful, even reassuring.

Transparent communication starts internally. Systems often rely on distributed components, microservices, databases, and APIs that interact across networks and platforms. When one part of the system degrades, it must inform its peers of this condition in a way that allows the system as a whole to adjust its behavior. This could involve rerouting traffic, invoking fallback mechanisms, or triggering rate-limiting policies. Without clear and timely internal signaling, systems can easily cascade from localized issues into broader outages. For example, if a database is under high load but does not flag this condition explicitly, application servers may continue to flood it with requests, pushing it past a recoverable state. Proper instrumentation and error signaling, communicating not just "failure" but degrees of performance degradation, enable systems to manage stress more gracefully and avoid compounding the problem.

Externally, failure transparency becomes even more critical. End users are often left in the dark when systems degrade, encountering generic error messages, spinning loaders, or worse, misleading signals that everything is functioning normally. This lack of clarity can lead to confusion, repeated failed actions, and ultimately, loss of confidence. A user who understands that a system is partially down, and why, is far more likely to stay engaged and give the system the benefit of the doubt. Even a brief, well-phrased message, "We're experiencing a temporary slowdown in processing uploads. You can continue working while we resolve the issue" can dramatically improve user experience in a failure scenario. The key is specificity, transparency, and tone. Users don't need every technical detail; they need enough context to understand what's affected, what they can or cannot do, and what the system is doing about it.

From the operator's perspective, transparency is about observability. It's not enough for systems to simply fail safely, they must do so visibly. This requires real-time monitoring, actionable alerts, and logs that go beyond cryptic error codes. Operators need insights into not just whether a component has failed, but how it's behaving, what conditions led to the degradation, and how close other components might be to similar stress. Failure transparency at this level enables rapid triage and minimizes mean time to recovery (MTTR). It also supports post-mortem analysis and continuous improvement, as clear failure signals help teams understand systemic weaknesses and prevent recurrence.

Importantly, the ability to communicate degraded states must be resilient. If the part of the system responsible for status updates or health checks goes down during an incident, users and operators are left without guidance at the exact moment they need it most. This is why many resilient systems decouple their status messaging infrastructure from the primary service path, using independent status pages, out-of-band communication channels, or lightweight health indicators that remain accessible even when core services falter. These auxiliary systems play a critical role in maintaining transparency when the primary system is impaired.

Failure transparency also has a broader cultural dimension. Organizations that value openness during incidents tend to recover more effectively and retain higher levels of customer loyalty. Hiding failures, or downplaying their impact, may offer short-term cover but almost always leads to longer-term consequences, loss of user trust, reputation damage, and internal friction. By contrast, systems and teams that acknowledge failures, communicate clearly, and demonstrate a plan for recovery cultivate credibility. Users may not love that something broke, but they'll appreciate being treated with honesty and respect.

Ultimately, failure is inevitable in any sufficiently complex system. What matters is how it's handled, and how it's communicated. Failure transparency transforms breakdowns from moments of frustration into opportunities for engagement, resilience, and trust-building. It allows systems to act not just as tools but as collaborators in the user's task, offering guidance even when things don't go according to plan. And in that, it becomes a vital part of the overall resilience strategy, one that bridges the technical with the human.

Internal State Communication

When components within a system can communicate their internal health and projected states, the system as a whole begins to function more like a living organism, one that can sense not just where it's hurting, but where it might hurt next, and take steps to minimize impact before the pain sets in. This kind of systemic self-awareness is critical in complex, distributed environments where local decisions made in isolation often lead to global dysfunction. When each component is blind to the health or capacity of others, the overall system becomes brittle, reacting too slowly or erratically to emerging stresses. By contrast, shared visibility into health and performance enables more nuanced and coordinated responses to stress, allowing the system to flex rather than break.

Health communication must go beyond simple binary states of "up" or "down." Systems need to express gradients of health, performance degradation, rising latency, and resource exhaustion trends, not just to alert others of failure, but to indicate when they're approaching thresholds where performance may be compromised. Standardized health reporting protocols are the foundation here. They provide a common language for expressing these conditions so that other components, regardless of their function or origin, can interpret and act on them. These protocols can take the form of structured heartbeats, service mesh health endpoints, or streaming telemetry data that reflects CPU load, memory pressure, queue sizes, error rates, and more. The important thing is consistency: everyone speaking and listening in the same way.

Real-time broadcasting of this data, whether via push notifications, message queues, or pub-sub systems, enables responsive behaviors. Components that are aware of degraded peers can reroute requests, throttle demand, or spin up compensating services before the situation becomes acute. This responsiveness is particularly critical in microservices architectures, where the failure or slowness of one component can ripple outward, causing cascading timeouts and backlogs. Subscription-based models further increase efficiency by letting components selectively listen to relevant state changes, rather than constantly polling for updates or parsing irrelevant noise.

The next evolution of internal state communication involves predictive elements. Rather than waiting for degradation to manifest fully before signaling distress, components can learn to anticipate their own decline based on telemetry trends. For instance, a database node observing rapidly increasing response times and disk I/O pressure might flag a likely near-future overload, allowing application services to begin throttling non-essential queries or shifting load to replicas. This kind of anticipatory signaling requires not only robust telemetry collection but also analytics engines capable of making short-term predictions with reasonable confidence. Machine learning models, statistical trend analysis, and threshold-based forecasting all play roles here, depending on the system's complexity and criticality.

The real value of predictive communication is that it smooths out the system's response curve. Instead of sharp transitions from healthy to degraded to failed, systems can begin adapting during the early phases of stress, allowing for more graceful handling. This minimizes the need for dramatic emergency interventions and preserves a higher quality of service under adverse conditions. It also prevents the "cliff effect," where performance suddenly collapses after crossing a threshold, catching other components off guard and accelerating cascading failures.

Crucially, these internal communications should be both observable and verifiable. Operators and diagnostic tools must be able to tap into this messaging to understand what's happening, why components are making the decisions they are, and where interventions may be needed. Logging, tracing, and metrics systems all benefit from access to this health signaling fabric, creating a richer, more interpretable picture of system behavior over time. This visibility also supports testing and validation of failure responses, ensuring that adaptive mechanisms aren't just coded but actually triggered under appropriate conditions.

Ultimately, coordinated degradation is about systems acting in concert, not in chaos. Health communication enables that coordination. It transforms a collection of independent parts into an interdependent whole, one capable of managing complexity through distributed intelligence and cooperative adaptation. The more clearly and consistently components can express their state, and the more intelligently others can interpret and act on that information, the more resilient the system becomes in practice, not just in theory.

User-Facing Failure Communication

When degradation occurs, clear communication with users transforms a potentially frustrating experience into a manageable one. Effective user-facing failure communication: Acknowledges the issue promptly rather than hiding or downplaying it Clearly explains what functionality is affected and what remains available Provides realistic expectations about duration and impact Offers actionable alternatives or workarounds when possible Updates users as conditions change or more information becomes available This transparent approach builds trust by treating users as partners in managing the degraded experience rather than victims of an unexplained failure. The most sophisticated failure communication adapts to both user context and failure severity. Critical users may receive more detailed information than casual ones; major outages warrant different communication approaches than minor degradations. This context-aware messaging ensures users receive information appropriate to their needs and circumstances.

Recovery-Oriented Computing: Designing for Rapid Restoration

Even the most elegantly degrading system must eventually recover to full functionality. Recovery-oriented computing designs systems not just to survive failures but to restore normal operation quickly and safely. This approach recognizes recovery as a first-class design concern rather than an afterthought, incorporating restoration capabilities directly into the system architecture.

Fast Restart and Initialization

Traditional systems often require lengthy startup procedures to initialize components, establish connections, warm caches, and reach optimal operating conditions. These extended initialization periods become major liabilities during recovery, extending outages and complicating restoration efforts. Recovery-oriented designs specifically optimize for fast restarts through:

Incremental initialization that allows components to begin processing work before fully initialized Prioritized startup sequences that restore critical functions before less essential one's Parallel initialization processes that reduce overall startup time Persistent caches that survive restarts and eliminate warm-up periods Configuration snapshots that eliminate time-consuming discovery processes

These optimizations can reduce recovery time from minutes or hours to seconds, dramatically improving system availability even when failures cannot be prevented.

Live Recovery and Hot Swapping

Live recovery and hot swapping represent the pinnacle of system resilience not just surviving failure but recovering so seamlessly that the end user never experiences a moment of interruption. These techniques move the system beyond reactive error handling into proactive continuity, where failures are anticipated and absorbed into the normal rhythm of operation. At this level of resilience, recovery is not an exception to the workflow but an integral part of it, blending into the background like a conductor adjusting tempo without disrupting the music.

To achieve this level of continuity, the system must be architected from the ground up with real-time adaptability in mind. At its core, live recovery requires the ability to detect component failures quickly and shift operational responsibilities without dropping requests or corrupting session state. This begins with the capability to replay or reprocess interrupted requests. When a failure occurs mid-transaction, the system must know which operations were successfully completed, which were not, and how to resume or rerun the necessary steps without duplication or data inconsistency. This means maintaining detailed transactional logs or checkpoints that can be used to reconstruct the user's path and finish the work as if nothing had happened. Without this level of traceability, seamless recovery becomes impossible.

Another crucial capability is connection management that can dynamically reroute traffic. This involves more than load balancing; it requires stateful awareness of which connections are active, which can be preserved, and where new destinations are viable. When a service instance fails, existing connections need to be handed off to replicas or standby instances, ideally without the client having to retry or reconnect. In many modern systems, this is enabled by service meshes or orchestration layers that manage service discovery and traffic routing, stepping in automatically when nodes go down. These layers must not only identify healthy targets but also understand session affinity, regional preferences, and real-time capacity constraints to make smart routing decisions on the fly.

Underpinning this orchestration is state transfer. Many services hold active user sessions, temporary data, or working memory that, if lost, would cause users to experience sudden terminations or restarts. State transfer mechanisms, whether in-memory replication, shared data stores, or distributed session caches, allow the system to migrate that information to a new component instance as part of the recovery flow. This enables features like "sticky sessions" or session persistence to survive the underlying failure. In real-time systems, this transfer must happen in milliseconds to maintain the illusion of uninterrupted service. It's a technical challenge that often relies on careful tuning of data consistency models, replication latency, and transactional guarantees.

Layered on top of these runtime considerations is the issue of version compatibility. For live recovery to support rolling updates or continuous deployment, components must be able to interoperate across versions during the upgrade process. This requires strict adherence to versioning protocols, backward-compatible APIs, and schema evolution strategies. Without these, a failed component cannot be safely replaced by a new one while others continue running an older code, and the recovery process introduces fragmentation or inconsistency. Designing with version agility in mind ensures that hot swapping can happen even as the system evolves, minimizing the traditional trade-off between availability and progress.

Though implementing live recovery is technically demanding, the payoff is massive. Systems that recover online and in real time can maintain near-continuous availability, a crucial requirement in environments where downtime translates directly into lost revenue, compromised safety, or customer attrition. Financial systems, medical platforms, telecom infrastructure, and high-traffic digital services all benefit from architectures that treat failure as routine rather than exceptional. Even in consumer-facing products, this level of resilience can elevate user trust and brand perception, making services feel reliable, professional, and always "on."

Perhaps the most important insight about live recovery is that it blurs the line between fault tolerance and graceful evolution. A system capable of hot-swapping a failed node can just as easily hot-swap a newly improved version of that node. This makes resilience and agility two sides of the same coin, supporting not just survival but growth and adaptation in dynamic environments. The more fluidly a system can handle change, whether triggered by failure or innovation, the better positioned it is for long-term success.

Learning from Failure: Postmortems and Continuous Improvement

The recovery process doesn't end when functionality is restored, it continues with structured analysis of what happened and how to prevent similar incidents in the future. This learning stage transforms each failure from a purely negative event into an opportunity for system improvement.

Focus on systemic issues rather than individual errors Identify not just the immediate technical causes but also contributing organizational factors Produce specific, actionable improvement recommendations Track implementation of these recommendations to ensure follow-through Share lessons learned across the organization to prevent similar failures elsewhere

These practices create a virtuous cycle where each failure leads to incremental improvements in both system design and operational practices, continuously increasing resilience over time.

Designing for Observability: You Can't Fix What You Can't See

Graceful degradation requires awareness; systems cannot respond appropriately to failures they cannot detect or understand. Observability, the ability to infer internal system states from external outputs, provides the visibility necessary for effective degradation management and rapid recovery.

Traditional monitoring focuses on predefined metrics and known failure modes. While valuable, this approach often misses novel or complex failures that don't trigger established thresholds. True observability goes beyond monitoring to enable exploration and investigation of unfamiliar patterns and unexpected behaviors.

Logs that provide detailed records of system events and actions Metrics that quantify system performance and behavior Traces that track request flows through distributed components State snapshots that capture point-in-time system conditions Dependency maps that visualize relationships between components

These complementary data sources enable operators to understand not just what is happening but why it's happening, providing the context needed for effective intervention during degraded operation.

Designing for Debuggability

Truly observable systems are designed from the ground up to facilitate debugging during failure conditions. This design philosophy incorporates capabilities like

Consistent correlation identifiers that track requests across component boundaries Structured logging with standardized formats and severity levels Exposed internal state that can be queried through management interfaces Introspection capabilities that allow components to report their own condition Configurable verbosity that can be increased during troubleshooting

These features transform debugging from an archaeological exercise of piecing together fragments of information into a surgical process of identifying and addressing specific issues, dramatically reducing mean time to recovery.

Operational Readiness: Preparing for Failure Response

Observability tools provide the raw materials for effective failure response, but organizations must also develop the operational practices and capabilities to use these tools effectively. This operational readiness encompasses Playbooks that document standard responses to common failure scenarios On-call rotations that ensure skilled responders are always available Escalation paths that bring in appropriate expertise for complex problems Regular exercises that practice failure response in realistic scenarios Post-incident reviews that continuously improve response procedures These human and process elements complement technical observability features to create a holistic approach to failure management.

Choosing the Right Level of Protection

Different components within a system warrant different levels of resilience investment based on their criticality, failure likelihood, and recovery complexity. Applying uniform resilience mechanisms across all components leads to either under-protection of critical functions or over-complication of simple ones.

Effective resilience design tailors' protection mechanisms to specific components based on

Criticality assessment using the categorization frameworks discussed earlier Failure impact analysis that quantifies the consequences of different failure modes Recovery complexity evaluation that identifies components with challenging restoration processes Resource constraints that limit the total complexity budget available for resilience features

This targeted approach focuses resilience investments where they deliver the greatest value, avoiding the diminishing returns of excessive protection mechanisms.

The graceful failure paradigm represents more than just a collection of technical patterns; it embodies a fundamental shift in how we think about system reliability and resilience. Rather than pursuing the impossible goal of preventing all failures, this approach accepts failure as inevitable and focuses on managing its impact through thoughtful design, transparent communication, and rapid recovery.

This philosophical shift has profound implications for how we design, build, and operate complex systems. It changes our success metrics from mean time between failures to mean time to recovery and service impact minimization. It transforms our architectural priorities from maximizing theoretical reliability to optimizing practical availability. And perhaps most importantly, it reframes our relationship with failure itself from an exceptional condition to be feared to a normal operational state to be managed.

The most resilient systems are not those that never fail, but those that fail in predictable, manageable ways, continuing to deliver value even as they operate in degraded states. By embracing this reality and designing accordingly, we create systems that remain reliable not despite failures but through them, turning inevitable disruptions from catastrophes into merely noticeable events.

CHAPTER FOUR

Refactoring Patterns for Robust Architecture

Legacy systems are everywhere. They power our banks, manage our healthcare data, control critical infrastructure, and facilitate countless everyday transactions. Many of these systems were built in eras before resilience was a primary design consideration, or they've evolved over time into brittle architectures that struggle to withstand modern pressures. Yet wholesale replacement is rarely feasible due to cost, risk, and business continuity requirements. Refactoring the process of restructuring existing systems while preserving external behavior offers a practical path toward enhanced resilience without the disruption of complete rewrites.

This chapter explores proven refactoring patterns that systematically transform brittle architectures into robust frameworks capable of withstanding today's demanding conditions. Unlike earlier chapters that focused on design principles for new systems, here we focus on pragmatic approaches to enhancing resilience in existing systems that cannot be rebuilt from scratch. Through these patterns, even the most fragile legacy architecture can evolve toward greater resilience while continuing to deliver business value.

We'll examine these patterns through multiple lenses, considering technical implementation details, organizational approaches, and real-world case studies that demonstrate successful application across diverse domains. Each pattern addresses specific resilience challenges, from reducing coupling and enhancing isolation to improving observability and enabling graceful degradation. Together, they provide a comprehensive toolkit for incrementally strengthening system resilience without disrupting essential services.

The Refactoring Mindset: Evolution, Not Revolution

Before diving into specific patterns, we must establish the proper mindset for resilience-oriented refactoring. This approach differs fundamentally from both greenfield development and traditional optimization-focused refactoring. It requires patience, strategic thinking, and a deep understanding of risk management.

The journey toward resilient architecture begins with accepting that transformation must be incremental, a series of carefully planned steps rather than a single dramatic leap. Just as the legendary ship of Theseus was gradually rebuilt plank by plank until no original material remained; resilient systems can emerge through incremental transformation of brittle ones. This approach replaces or enhances components individually while maintaining system functionality, gradually increasing resilience without disrupting operations.

Successful incremental transformation requires careful sequencing of modifications. We must identify components with the highest fragility-to-effort ratio, those where modest refactoring yields substantial resilience improvements. By addressing these high-leverage points first, we build momentum while demonstrating value, essential for sustaining organizational commitment to long-term refactoring initiatives.

The incremental approach also creates natural checkpoints where progress can be evaluated, and strategies adjusted based on observed outcomes. This feedback loop prevents the refactoring equivalent of "big bang" deployments, where massive changes introduced simultaneously often lead to unexpected complications and rollbacks.

In medical practice, "primum non nocere", first, do no harm, reminds physicians that interventions carry risks and must be approached with caution. The same principle applies to resilience refactoring, where well-intentioned changes can inadvertently introduce new vulnerabilities or trigger latent issues in interconnected components.

Risk-aware refactoring incorporates comprehensive testing strategies, gradual deployments, and rollback mechanisms that limit potential damage. It acknowledges that increasing resilience in one dimension (like scalability) may temporarily decrease it in another (like operational familiarity), requiring careful balancing of immediate and long-term risks.

This mindset also recognizes that some components may be too fragile or critical to refactor directly. In such cases, indirect approaches, wrapping fragile components in protective layers, building redundant alternatives, or implementing circuit breakers may provide resilience benefits without modifying high-risk code.

Just as financial debt accumulates interest over time, technical debt creates growing burdens on development and operations. Resilience debt, the accumulated fragility resulting from expedient but brittle design choices, similarly compounds over time, making systems increasingly vulnerable to disruption and increasingly resistant to improvement.

Understanding the relationship between technical debt and resilience debt is crucial for effective refactoring. Some forms of technical debt directly impact resilience and warrant immediate attention. Others may have minimal resilience implications and can be addressed later or even tolerated indefinitely if resources are limited.

Decoupling Patterns: Breaking Harmful Dependencies

Dense, unmanaged dependencies lie at the heart of many resilience issues. When components are tightly coupled, failures propagate rapidly through the system, transforming localized issues into widespread outages. Decoupling patterns systematically reduce these harmful dependencies, creating natural boundaries that contain failures and enable independent evolution of components.

The Strangler Fig pattern, named after the tropical vine, that gradually envelops and replaces its host tree, offers a low-risk approach to replacing brittle components with more resilient alternatives. Rather than modifying the fragile component directly, this pattern creates a new implementation with improved resilience characteristics, gradually redirects traffic from the old implementation to the new one, maintains both implementations during the transition period, and eventually removes the original implementation when it no longer receives traffic.

This approach minimizes risk by allowing easy rollback at any point during the transition. It also enables incremental migration, with specific transaction types or user segments moving to the new implementation while others continue using the original until confidence in the replacement grows.

replace a monolithic trading platform built in the 1990s. Rather than attempting a high-risk cutover, they built resilient microservice replacements for specific trading functions, using an API gateway to route requests appropriately. Over two years, they migrated all functionality without any significant outages, ultimately decommissioning a system that had previously been considered too risky to modify.

When legacy components cannot be immediately replaced but present resilience risks, the Anti-Corruption Layer pattern creates a buffer between these components and the rest of the system. This intermediate layer translates between modern and legacy interfaces and protocols, handles error conditions from the legacy component gracefully, implements resilience mechanisms like circuit breakers and timeouts, and provides logging and instrumentation absent from the legacy implementation.

Unlike the Strangler Fig, which replaces functionality, the Anti-Corruption Layer preserves the legacy component while mitigating its resilience impact on the broader system. This pattern is particularly valuable when the legacy component works correctly under normal conditions but behaves unpredictably under stress or failure scenarios.

A healthcare provider needed to continue using a critical patient data system that lacked modern resilience features. They implemented an anti-corruption layer that cached frequently accessed data, implemented circuit breakers to prevent cascading failures during outages, and provided graceful degradation options not available in the original system. This approach improved overall system resilience without modifying the risky legacy code.

Many brittle systems suffer from unclear responsibility boundaries, with components entangled in ways that make isolation impossible. Domain Boundary Enforcement refactors these systems by identifying coherent functional domains within the existing architecture, establishing clear contracts and interfaces between domains, refactoring code to eliminate cross-domain implementation dependencies, and creating dedicated communication channels between domains.

This pattern reduces coupling by ensuring that domains interact only through well-defined interfaces rather than through shared implementation details or backdoor dependencies. The resulting boundaries create natural bulkheads that limit failure propagation while also improving system comprehensibility and maintainability.

Resilience Layer Patterns: Adding Protection Mechanisms

Sometimes the fastest path to improved resilience involves adding protective layers around existing components rather than modifying them directly. Resilience Layer patterns introduce these protective mechanisms with minimal disruption to core functionality, creating immediate resilience benefits while enabling more comprehensive refactoring over time.

The Circuit Breaker pattern prevents cascade failures by temporarily suspending calls to failing components. Unlike simpler timeout mechanisms, circuit breakers track failure rates over time and "trip" when they exceed defined thresholds, preventing further calls until the component shows signs of recovery. This pattern identifies service dependencies suitable for circuit breaker protection, implements failure detection with appropriate thresholds and trip conditions, provides fallback mechanisms for use when the circuit is open, and includes automatic recovery testing to restore normal operation when appropriate.

Adding circuit breakers requires minimal changes to existing components, making this pattern an excellent starting point for resilience refactoring. The resulting protection immediately improves system stability while providing valuable data about component reliability that can inform subsequent refactoring priorities.

An e-commerce platform frequently experienced complete outages when their product review service became overloaded. By implementing circuit breakers around calls to this service, they prevented these localized issues from affecting the critical purchasing flow. The detailed telemetry from the circuit breakers later informed a more comprehensive refactoring of the review service itself, addressing the root causes of its instability.

Named after the watertight compartments in ship hulls that prevent flooding from sinking the entire vessel, the bulkhead pattern isolates components to contain failure and resource consumption. Retrofitting bulkheads into existing systems separates components into distinct process spaces or containers, allocates dedicated resource pools to each component, implements governance mechanisms that enforce resource limits, and prevents resource exhaustion in one component from affecting others.

This pattern requires minimal changes to component internals, focusing instead on how they're deployed and how resources are allocated to them. The resulting isolation provides immediate resilience benefits by preventing resource contention issues that often trigger cascading failures.

A media streaming service experienced regular outages when recommendation processing consumed excessive database connections, preventing user authentication from functioning. By implementing connection pool bulkheads that guaranteed minimum resources for authentication flows, they maintained core functionality even when recommendation systems misbehaved, buying time for more comprehensive refactoring of the resource-hungry components.

Timeout management patterns address how systems handle unresponsive dependencies. Many resilience issues stem from inadequate timeout handling, where unresponsive dependencies block threads indefinitely, eventually exhausting resources. Comprehensive timeout management audits all external calls to identify missing or inadequate timeouts, implements appropriate timeout values based on operational patterns, adds timeout handling logic with clear fallback behaviors, and creates monitoring for timeout frequency to identify problematic dependencies.

State Management Patterns: Preserving Critical Information

State management controls how systems maintain and recover information and profoundly impacts resilience. Brittle systems often store state in ways that create single points of failure or complicate recovery. State management refactoring patterns transform these vulnerable approaches into more resilient alternatives without disrupting system functionality.

Event sourcing retrofits transform traditional state storage approaches by storing the sequence of events that produced the current state, enabling reconstruction if the state store fails. This pattern identifies critical states that warrant event-based durability, adds event logging alongside traditional state updates, implements reconstruction capabilities that rebuild state from event histories, and eventually transitions from state-based to event-based primacy where appropriate.

This pattern initially supplements rather than replaces existing state management, providing an additional resilience layer without disrupting current operations. Over time, the event log may become the authoritative source of truth, enabling more sophisticated resilience and scaling patterns.

An insurance claims processing system-maintained policy information in a relational database that occasionally corrupted during high-load periods. By retrofitting event sourcing, they captured all policy changes as immutable events, enabling accurate reconstruction when corruption occurred. This approach eliminated data loss incidents while they developed a more comprehensive redesign of their policy management system.

State partitioning addresses the risks of monolithic datastores by dividing them into smaller, more focused datastores that can fail independently. Many legacy systems store all state in monolithic databases that create single points of failure and scalability bottlenecks. State partitioning refactors these monoliths by analyzing data access patterns to identify natural partitioning boundaries, implementing data access layers that support multiple backing stores, migrating data in phases from monolithic to partitioned storage, and updating application logic to work with the partitioned model.

This pattern improves resilience by ensuring that failures affect only specific data partitions rather than the entire state store. It also enables different resilience strategies for different data types based on their criticality and access patterns.

A telecommunications provider maintained all customer data in a single database instance that repeatedly caused system-wide outages during maintenance operations. By partitioning customer data by region and service type, they contained failures to specific customer segments while enabling targeted recovery operations. This approach dramatically improved overall system availability while paving the way for more sophisticated multi-region resilience strategies.

Observability Refactoring: Making the Invisible Visible

Many legacy systems operate as black boxes, providing minimal visibility into their internal operations and making troubleshooting nearly impossible during incidents. Observability refactoring transforms these opaque systems into transparent ones that expose their internal state, behavior, and health, enabling more effective monitoring, faster diagnosis, and proactive intervention before failures occur.

The telemetry injection pattern adds comprehensive instrumentation to existing systems without modifying their core functionality. This pattern identifies key monitoring points within the existing architecture, implements non-invasive instrumentation techniques that capture critical metrics and events, creates standardized output formats that integrate with modern observability platforms, and establishes baseline behaviors for detecting anomalies.

This approach transforms previously opaque systems into observable ones without the risk of modifying business logic. The resulting visibility enables earlier detection of emerging issues, more precise diagnosis of failures, and data-driven prioritization of subsequent resilience improvements.

A government agency operated a critical benefits processing system with minimal internal visibility, often learning of problems only from user complaints. By implementing telemetry injection at key integration points, they gained real-time visibility into system behavior without modifying the sensitive core logic. This visibility enabled them to detect and address issues before they affected users, dramatically improving service quality while building the understanding needed for more comprehensive refactoring.

Health models transform raw telemetry into actionable health assessments by establishing clear definitions of what constitutes "healthy" operation. The health model pattern implements structured health reporting across system components, defines multi-dimensional health criteria beyond simple "up/down" status, creates aggregation mechanisms that produce system-level health assessments from component-level signals, and implements health-based routing and failover mechanisms.

This pattern transforms vague notions of system health into precise, actionable metrics that enable automated responses to degrading conditions. The resulting clarity supports both immediate resilience improvements through automated interventions and longer-term refactoring priorities based on observed health patterns.

A financial trading platform struggled with unpredictable performance degradations that were difficult to detect and diagnose. By implementing comprehensive health models, they established clear definitions of health across latency, error rates, and throughput dimensions. These models enabled automatic detection of degrading conditions and triggered remediation actions before users experienced significant impact, creating time for operators to implement permanent solutions.

Distributed tracing retrofits add request-level visibility to complex distributed systems by tracking request flows across component boundaries. This pattern implements correlation identifier propagation throughout the system, adds span recording at key processing points, creates visualization tools that reconstruct end-to-end request flows, and enables performance analysis across component boundaries.

This approach transforms opaque distributed interactions into transparent, traceable flows that can be analyzed and optimized. The resulting visibility facilitates both immediate troubleshooting during incidents and targeted refactoring to address structural resilience issues.

A retail company's order processing system spanned dozens of services with no end-to-end visibility, making it nearly impossible to diagnose intermittent failures. By implementing distributed tracing, they gained the ability to follow specific orders through the entire processing flow, quickly identifying bottlenecks and failure points. This visibility not only shortened incident resolution times but also informed architectural improvements that eliminated common failure patterns.

The refactoring patterns explored in this chapter provide practical approaches to transforming brittle systems into resilient ones without the risks of complete rewrites. By applying these patterns systematically, organizations can gradually increase system resilience while continuing to deliver business value.

The most successful refactoring initiatives combine these technical patterns with organizational practices that support continuous resilience improvement. These include dedicated refactoring time allocations, incremental funding models that recognize resilience as a core investment rather than overhead, and metrics that demonstrate the business value of resilience improvements through reduced outages and faster recovery times.

As systems evolve through these refactoring patterns, they become not just more resilient but also more amenable to further improvement. The decoupling, protection mechanisms, state management improvements, and observability enhancements create a foundation for ongoing evolution toward ever greater resilience.

The journey from brittle to robust architecture is never truly complete. As technologies evolve, user expectations increase, and business demands change, new resilience challenges continuously emerge. The patterns in this chapter establish not just immediate improvements but sustainable processes for continuous resilience evolution that can adapt to these changing requirements.

CHAPTER FIVE

Distributed Resilience Beyond Single Points of Failure

The fundamental weakness of centralized systems lies in their inherent architectural vulnerability. When critical functionality concentrates on a single component, location, or process, the entire system becomes susceptible to catastrophic failure. This vulnerability manifests across diverse domains, from information technology infrastructure to supply chains, energy grids, and organizational structures. Consider the fragility of a metropolitan area dependent on a single water treatment facility, a global corporation whose operations rely on a centralized data center, or a national economy overly dependent on a specific industry sector. These configurations represent classic single points of failure, where disruption to one element can trigger exponential consequences throughout interconnected systems.

Historical examples abound: the 2003 Northeast blackout that affected 55 million people originated from failures in a single utility company's monitoring system; the 2011 Thailand floods disrupted global hard drive production by affecting facilities responsible for nearly 45% of worldwide capacity; and the 2021 Suez Canal blockage by a single container ship impacted approximately 12% of global trade. In each case, the concentration of critical functionality created vulnerability disproportionate to the initial triggering event.

The evolution toward centralization often follows a predictable pattern driven by economic and organizational incentives. Consolidation reduces operational overhead, simplifies coordination, minimizes redundancy costs, and creates economies of scale. Centralized systems typically demonstrate superior efficiency under normal operating conditions, creating short-term competitive advantages. However, this optimization frequently comes at the expense of long-term resilience, introducing systemic risk that remains invisible until activated by disruption. This fundamental tension between operational efficiency and systemic resilience represents one of the core dilemmas in modern infrastructure and organizational design.

Centralization also concentrates decision-making authority, potentially creating bottlenecks during crisis response when adaptability becomes paramount. When disruption occurs, centralized systems often face compound challenges: not only must they address the technical or operational failure, but they must also overcome communication and coordination constraints imposed by their hierarchical structure. The resulting response delays can transform manageable disturbances into system-wide failures as cascading effects accelerate beyond control thresholds.

Distributed Architectures: The Path to Resilience

Distributed resilience fundamentally reimagines system architecture by dispersing functionality, authority, and resources across multiple independent but interconnected nodes. Rather than concentrating critical capabilities within singular components or locations, distributed systems intentionally spread essential functions throughout networks of semi-autonomous elements. This architectural paradigm draws inspiration from biological systems, like neural networks or immune responses, that maintain functionality even when individual components fail.

The internet provides a quintessential example of distributed architecture, originally conceived through DARPA research as a communication system resistant to nuclear attack. Its foundational protocol suite (TCP/IP) enables packet routing around damaged infrastructure, allowing the network to maintain connectivity despite significant disruption. Modern cloud computing extends this philosophy through technologies like sharded databases that distribute information across multiple physical locations, container orchestration platforms that dynamically reallocate computational workloads when servers fail, and content delivery networks that replicate data across global edge locations to maintain availability despite regional outages.

Beyond digital infrastructure, distributed principles increasingly influence physical systems. Modern electrical grid design incorporates microgrids capable of disconnecting from the broader network during disturbances, maintaining local service through distributed generation. Supply chain resilience strategies now emphasize geographic diversification of manufacturing capacity, multi-sourcing of critical components, and nearshoring production to reduce dependence on extended logistics networks. Financial systems implement distributed ledger technologies that eliminate vulnerable central clearinghouses while maintaining transaction integrity through cryptographic consensus mechanisms.

Redundancy provides multiple instances of critical components, ensuring functionality persists when individual elements fail. However, true resilience requires going beyond simple redundancy to incorporate diversity, variations in implementation, technology stacks, geographic location, and vulnerability profiles. This diversity ensures that problems affecting one class of components won't simultaneously compromise all redundant elements.

Modularity establishes clear boundaries between system components, limiting failure propagation through well-defined interfaces. When modules can be replaced or bypassed without disrupting the entire system, overall resilience increases substantially. Effective distributed architectures also incorporate graceful degradation capabilities, allowing systems to maintain core functionality at reduced performance levels rather than experiencing binary failure states.

Coordination Without Control: Governance in Distributed Systems

The distribution of functionality across semi-autonomous nodes creates fundamental governance challenges. Traditional command-and-control structures become increasingly ineffective as authority and capability disperse throughout the system. Successful distributed architectures therefore develop alternative coordination mechanisms that maintain system coherence without reimposing centralized vulnerabilities.

Distributed consensus protocols represent one class of these coordination mechanisms. Bitcoin's blockchain implementation demonstrates how thousands of independent nodes can achieve agreement on transaction validity without central authority through proof-of-work consensus. Enterprise-grade distributed systems often employ more sophisticated approaches like Practical Byzantine Fault Tolerance (PBFT) or Raft consensus algorithms that balance performance requirements with resilience against both accidental failures and malicious attacks.

Open-source software communities provide instructive examples of distributed governance at scale. The Linux kernel, supporting critical infrastructure worldwide, develops through a distributed collaboration model where thousands of contributors coordinate without traditional management hierarchies. Instead, the community relies on shared technical standards, transparent peer review processes, meritocratic influence structures, and modularity that allows parallel work streams. Similar approaches appear in Wikipedia's distributed knowledge production, OpenStreetMap's collaborative cartography, and scientific research communities' peer review systems.

Federated decision-making structures offer another governance approach for distributed systems. The federation maintains local autonomy while establishing protocols for cross-boundary coordination and resource sharing. The European Union exemplifies political federation, balancing member state sovereignty with coordination mechanisms addressing transnational challenges. In technology contexts, federated architectures appear in email systems (SMTP protocol connecting independent mail servers), social media alternatives (Mastodon's federated instance model), and identity management systems (SAML and OAuth federations).

Effective distributed governance frequently incorporates incentive alignment mechanisms ensuring that autonomous nodes, acting in self-interest, collectively produce desired system-wide outcomes. Cryptocurrency networks incentivize security contributions through mining rewards and transaction fees. Open-source ecosystems develop sustainability through reputation economies, corporate sponsorship models, and foundation support. These incentive structures replace direct control with indirect influence, maintaining system integrity through carefully designed feedback loops rather than centralized enforcement mechanisms.

The Human Element: Cultural and Organizational Factors

The technological architecture of distributed systems represents only part of resilience engineering. Equally crucial are the human systems, organizational structures, and cultural practices that determine how distributed technologies perform under pressure. Organizations successful in building distributed resilience cultivate specific organizational mindsets: comfort with controlled ambiguity, willingness to trade short-term efficiency for long-term robustness, and valuing preparedness over optimization.

High-reliability organizations (HROs) operating in domains where failure could prove catastrophic, such as nuclear power generation, air traffic control, and spacecraft operations, demonstrate these principles consistently. Despite working with complex technologies in unpredictable environments, these organizations maintain remarkable safety records through cultural and organizational practices that distribute authority and expertise. They maintain sensitivity to operations through practices like regular cross-functional huddles, enable rapid anomaly response by empowering front-line decision-making, and cultivate preoccupation with failure through near-miss reporting systems and regular simulation exercises.

Naval operations aboard aircraft carriers exemplify these principles in action. Despite extreme time pressure and potential catastrophic consequences, carrier flight decks demonstrate exceptional reliability through distributed organizational practices. Authority distributes according to expertise rather than rank during critical operations. Communication protocols emphasize information sharing across hierarchy levels. Training emphasizes adaptive response to unexpected conditions rather than rote procedure following. These cultural and organizational patterns prove as important to resilience as the redundant technical systems aboard the vessel.

Distributed resilience requires rethinking traditional management approaches that prioritize centralized control, standardization, and efficiency optimization. Rather than treating variation as deviation requiring correction, resilient systems often benefit from controlled diversity that provides adaptive capacity during disruption. Rather than eliminating all spare capacity in pursuit of lean operations, they maintain strategic reserves and alternative pathways that appear "wasteful" during normal operations but become essential during disruption. These cultural shifts often prove more challenging than implementing distributed technical architectures, requiring fundamental reconsideration of values and priorities that may conflict with established business practices and metrics.

Knowledge distribution represents another critical human factor in resilient systems. Organizations building distributed resilience intentionally avoid knowledge concentration through practices like cross-training, detailed documentation, skill redundancy, and communities of practice. They recognize that resilience depends not only on distributing technical functionality but also on ensuring that critical understanding and capabilities exist throughout the organization rather than residing exclusively with individual "irreplaceable experts."

Implementation Challenges and Future Horizons

Transitioning from centralized to distributed architectures presents substantial challenges across technical, economic, organizational, and cultural dimensions. Legacy systems designed around centralized paradigms resist transformation due to technical interdependencies, organizational inertia, and sunk costs. Distributed approaches often impose higher operational complexity, increased coordination overhead, and reduced efficiency during normal operations. The benefits of resilience remain hypothetical until disruption occurs, making investment difficult to justify through traditional cost-benefit analysis focused on steady-state optimization.

Technical implementation challenges include managing increased system complexity, ensuring consistency across distributed components, designing appropriate failure detection mechanisms, and balancing autonomy with coordination. Organizations implementing distributed architectures must develop new monitoring approaches that provide visibility into distributed system states without recreating centralized vulnerabilities. They must also navigate the complexity of partial failure conditions where system components degrade rather than fail completely which can prove more challenging to detect and remediate than binary failure states.

Despite these challenges, several converging trends accelerate the shift toward distributed resilience. Climate change increases the frequency and severity of extreme events that stress centralized infrastructure. Geopolitical tensions raise concerns about supply chain vulnerabilities and critical resource dependencies. Modern digital technologies dramatically reduce coordination costs that historically favor centralization, enabling distributed collaboration at unprecedented scale and speed. Combined, these forces create both necessity and opportunity for distributed approaches across domains.

Emerging technologies further expand distributed resilience possibilities. Edge computing pushes processing capability to network peripheries, reducing dependence on centralized data centers. Mesh networks establish resilient communication infrastructure through peer-to-peer connectivity rather than hub-and-spoke architectures. Advanced cryptographic techniques enable secure collaboration without trusted central authorities. Artificial intelligence applications increasingly incorporate federated learning approaches that build collective intelligence while maintaining data sovereignty across distributed nodes.

The frontier of distributed resilience extends beyond traditional technical domains into social, economic, and political systems. Social movements increasingly adopt networked organizational structures resistant to disruption through leadership targeting or central resource control. Economic systems explore models that distribute financial risk rather than concentrating it in systemically important institutions. Democratic governance experiments with deliberative processes that distribute decision influence beyond representative structures. In each domain, core principles remain consistent: distribute critical functions to avoid single points of failure, embrace controlled diversity to enhance adaptive capacity, coordinate without centralizing control, and design for graceful degradation rather than binary success/failure states.

As our world grows increasingly complex and interconnected, the limitations of centralized approaches become more apparent. The compounding challenges of climate destabilization, resource constraints, geopolitical realignment, and technological acceleration create environments where disruption becomes inevitable. In this context, resilience through distribution emerges not merely as a technical design principle but as a fundamental philosophy for sustainable system design across technological, organizational, and social domains. The future belongs to architectures that embrace complexity through distribution rather than attempting to control it through centralization, creating systems capable of adaptation, learning, and persistence through unprecedented challenges.

CHAPTER SIX

Human Factors in System Resilience

System resilience, or the ability to anticipate, withstand, recover from, and adapt to adverse conditions, has become a top priority in industries ranging from healthcare and aviation to nuclear power and financial services. While technological solutions and organizational procedures contribute significantly to resilience, the human element often determines whether a system bends or breaks under pressure. This chapter explores the multifaceted ways human factors influence system resilience and how organizations can harness human capabilities to create more robust systems capable of weathering both anticipated and unanticipated challenges.

The Human as Both Vulnerability and Strength

The human component in complex systems presents a fundamental paradox that resilience engineers must address. On one hand, human error contributes to approximately 70-80% of industrial accidents and system failures, according to analyses across multiple industries. Cognitive limitations, including attention constraints, working memory capacity, and information processing bottlenecks, create vulnerabilities in system operation. Fatigue from extended work hours or disrupted circadian rhythms impair decision-making and vigilance, while stress narrows attentional focus and degrades performance on complex tasks. Decision-making biases, such as confirmation bias (seeking information that confirms existing beliefs) and availability heuristic (overweighting easily recalled information), can lead operators astray during critical situations.

On the other hand, humans possess remarkable adaptability, creativity, and problem-solving capabilities that automated systems cannot match. When Air Transat Flight 236 experienced complete fuel exhaustion over the Atlantic Ocean in 2001, Captain Robert Piché and First Officer Dirk DeJager successfully glided the Airbus A330 over 65 nautical miles to an emergency landing in the Azores, a feat no automated system could have accomplished. During the 2003 Northeast blackout affecting 55 million people, power plant operators in unaffected regions implemented creative load-balancing strategies that prevented the cascading failure from spreading further.

Understanding this duality is essential for resilience engineering. Rather than viewing humans merely as "weak links" to be controlled through rigid procedures, effective resilience strategies recognize human operators as adaptive resources capable of detecting anomalies, managing unexpected events, and implementing novel solutions when standard protocols fall short. The concept of "requisite imagination" highlights this human capacity to envision what might go wrong and develop creative countermeasures, a capability no algorithm currently possesses.

High-reliability organizations like aircraft carriers and nuclear submarines demonstrate that these organizations succeed not by eliminating human judgment but by cultivating it through training, organizational structures, and technologies that enhance human capabilities. Nuclear submarine crews regularly practice scenarios that go beyond standard operating procedures, developing what experts call a "hunter's mindset" that actively searches for subtle indicators of emerging problems.

Cognitive Foundations of Resilient Performance

The cognitive processes that enable resilient performance to deserve careful examination. Situation awareness, or the perception of environmental elements, comprehension of their meaning, and prediction of their future status, is the foundation of effective human response in critical situations. When operators maintain strong situational awareness, they can detect subtle warning signs of impending failure and take preventative action before things worsen.

Situation awareness operates on three levels: perception (Level 1), comprehension (Level 2), and projection (Level 3). At Level 1, operators must accurately perceive relevant system states and environmental factors. Commercial aviation incidents show that approximately 76% of situation awareness errors occur at this fundamental level, often due to information overload or attentional narrowing under stress. At Level 2, operators integrate perceived information into a coherent understanding of the current situation. This process draws heavily on domain expertise and mental models developed through experience. Level 3 involves projecting future states based on current understanding, anticipating how the situation will evolve, and planning accordingly.

Mental models, or internal representations of how systems function, have a significant impact on resilience. Accurate and flexible mental models help operators predict system behavior, recognize anomalies, and develop effective responses. Nuclear power operators with comprehensive mental models of plant thermodynamics respond more effectively to novel scenarios than those with fragmented, procedure-based knowledge. Training that enhances these mental models proves particularly valuable for resilience.

Domain-specific mental models enable what cognitive scientists call "recognition-primed decision making," the ability to rapidly recognize patterns from past experience and apply appropriate responses without deliberate analysis of alternatives. This process explains how experienced firefighters can make seemingly intuitive yet highly effective decisions when confronting unique fire scenarios. Experienced commanders typically consider only a single option based on pattern recognition rather than comparing multiple alternatives, an approach that proves remarkably effective in time-critical situations.

Working memory limitations significantly constrain human performance during complex operations. The typical capacity of 5-9 chunks of information can be quickly overwhelmed during emergency situations. Resilient systems accommodate these limitations through thoughtful interface design, cognitive offloading tools (like checklists and decision aids), and team structures that distribute cognitive load. Aviation's introduction of electronic checklists has reduced procedural errors by approximately 46% compared to paper checklists by reducing working memory demands.

Expertise development follows predictable stages from rule-based novice performance to intuitive expert performance with important implications for resilience. While novices rely heavily on explicit procedures and rules, experts develop perceptual skills that allow them to detect subtle patterns and anomalies. This "perceptual differentiation" enables experts to notice small deviations before they escalate into major problems. Experienced power plant operators detect approximately 70% more early warning signs than novices, often through subtle cues like unusual sounds or vibrations that automated systems miss entirely.

Social Dimensions of System Resilience

Resilience rarely manifests as an individual achievement but emerges through collective action across organizational levels. Team dynamics, communication patterns, and organizational culture profoundly influence how effectively human capabilities contribute to system resilience.

High-reliability organizations cultivate what safety experts call "collective mindfulness," a shared attentiveness to operational details and potential failures. This mindfulness manifests through five key processes: preoccupation with failure (continuously searching for potential problems), reluctance to simplify interpretations (appreciating the complexity of situations), sensitivity to operations (maintaining awareness of frontline activities), commitment to resilience (developing capabilities to detect and recover from errors), and deference to expertise (respecting knowledge rather than hierarchical authority).

Team coordination mechanisms significantly impact resilience. Explicit coordination through verbal communication works well in routine situations but becomes fragile during high-stress events. Implicit coordination, where team members anticipate each other's needs and actions based on shared mental models, proves more robust during emergencies. Surgical teams with strong implicit coordination experience, approximately 30% fewer adverse events during unexpected complications compared to teams relying solely on explicit coordination.

Communication practices significantly impact resilience. Effective teams maintain clear, concise communication during normal operations and adapt their communication strategies during crises. The adoption of standardized communication protocols like SBAR (Situation, Background, Assessment, Recommendation) in healthcare has reduced communication-related adverse events by up to 40% in some hospitals. Closed-loop communication, where receivers acknowledge messages and confirm understanding, proves particularly valuable during high-stress situations, reducing miscommunication by approximately 50%, according to simulation studies.

Power dynamics and psychological safety also influence resilience. Organizations where junior staff hesitate to voice concerns due to steep authority gradients become vulnerable to preventable failures. The 1977 Tenerife airport disaster, where a junior crew member's tentative warnings went unheeded before the deadliest collision in aviation history, tragically illustrates this principle. Conversely, organizations that cultivate psychological safety where people feel comfortable expressing concerns without fear of embarrassment or retribution demonstrate enhanced resilience through early problem identification and broader engagement in problem-solving.

Healthcare teams with high psychological safety report nearly three times as many minor errors and near misses compared to low psychological safety teams, not because they make more errors, but because they surface and address problems before they escalate. Similarly, organizational studies have found psychological safety to be the most significant predictor of team effectiveness across various performance metrics.

Organizational learning processes significantly influence resilience. Organizations vary dramatically in how they respond to failures, from defensive routines that obscure problems to generative approaches that treat failures as learning opportunities. Effective learning mechanisms include structured debriefs (like After Action Reviews), anonymous reporting systems, and cross-organizational learning networks. The aviation industry's confidential reporting systems exemplify this approach, collecting over 1.5 million confidential reports over decades and contributing to a dramatic reduction in commercial aviation accident rates.

Designing for Human-Centered Resilience

System design significantly influences how effectively human capabilities contribute to resilience. Traditional approaches often emphasize restricting human discretion through automation and rigid procedures. While these strategies can prevent certain errors, they may inadvertently undermine resilience by reducing operators' ability to adapt to unexpected situations.

Human-centered design for resilience acknowledges that perfect prediction of all potential failure modes is impossible. Instead, it focuses on creating systems that enhance human adaptive capacity. This includes designing interfaces that support situation awareness through appropriate information presentation, workstations that mitigate fatigue and stress, and automation that complements rather than replaces human capabilities.

Interface design profoundly influences resilience through its impact on situation awareness. Effective interfaces make system status and relevant parameters immediately apparent without requiring operators to integrate information from multiple sources. Ecological interface design, representing system constraints and relationships graphically, reduces detection time for abnormal conditions by approximately 40% compared to conventional displays. The redesign of nuclear power plant control rooms after Three Mile Island exemplifies this approach, with integrated overview displays that support rapid situation assessment during abnormal conditions.

Workstation ergonomics contribute significantly to human performance during extended operations. Factors like lighting, noise levels, temperature, and physical comfort influence vigilance and decision-making quality. Poorly designed bridge layouts contribute to approximately 23% of maritime collision incidents through their effects on operator fatigue and communication barriers. Effective designs consider not just individual workstations but also team interaction patterns and information flow requirements.

Automation design critically influences system resilience. Poorly designed automation creates new vulnerabilities through phenomena like mode confusion (uncertainty about what the automation is doing), skill degradation (erosion of manual skills), and automation complacency (over-reliance on automated systems). The "glass cockpit" evolution in aviation illustrates this progression, moving from early automation that confused pilots during mode transitions to more transparent systems that better support pilot awareness and intervention.

The concept of "human-automation teaming" represents a significant advancement in resilience engineering. Rather than treating automation as a replacement for human judgment, this approach envisions automation as a team player that handles routine tasks consistently while keeping humans informed and engaged, provides decision support without forcing specific actions, and gracefully degrades during failures rather than abruptly transferring control to unprepared operators. Cooperative automation designs lead to approximately 60% better anomaly detection compared to traditional automation approaches.

Physical environments also influence resilience through their effects on team coordination and communication. Control room layouts that facilitate visual contact between team members, shared displays that support common ground, and spaces that accommodate both focused individual work and team collaboration enhance collective performance during unexpected events. Emergency operations centers with layouts supporting dynamic reconfiguration based on incident requirements improve coordination effectiveness by approximately 35% compared to fixed layouts.

Building Resilient Human Capabilities

Resilience ultimately depends on developing human capabilities that enable adaptation to both anticipated and unanticipated challenges. Traditional training approaches focusing solely on procedural compliance prove insufficient for complex, dynamic environments. Instead, organizations must cultivate adaptive expertise, the ability to apply knowledge flexibly in novel situations.

Simulation-based training offers powerful opportunities to develop adaptive expertise. Rather than focusing exclusively on anticipated scenarios, effective simulations progressively introduce unexpected complications that require improvisation. Healthcare has embraced this approach through high-fidelity simulations that prepare medical teams not just for common emergencies but for complex, evolving situations that require adaptation and creativity. Teams trained with variable scenarios demonstrate approximately 40% better performance when confronting novel problems compared to teams trained on standardized scenarios.

The concept of "perturbation training" has proven particularly effective for building resilience capabilities. This approach deliberately introduces unexpected complications during training scenarios, forcing trainees to adapt rather than simply execute memorized procedures. Aviation crews who experience perturbation training handle novel emergency scenarios approximately 55% more effectively than those receiving conventional training, particularly in scenarios requiring departure from standard procedures.

Expertise development requires deliberate practice, not just repetition, but structured learning with clear goals, immediate feedback, and progressive challenge. Organizations that systematically incorporate deliberate practice into training programs develop personnel with greater adaptive capacity. Air traffic control training programs that incorporate deliberate practice principles produce controllers who handle approximately 32% more traffic during peak periods while maintaining safety margins.

Decision-making training specifically focused on uncertainty management enhances resilience. Techniques like "pre-mortem" analysis (imagining a future failure and working backward to identify causes) and "risk-based thinking" (systematically identifying what could go wrong) develop cognitive skills essential for resilience. Teams trained in uncertainty management techniques identify approximately 27% more potential failure modes before an operation and respond more effectively when unexpected events occur.

Experience-based learning also builds resilience capabilities. Organizations that systematically analyze both failures and successes create valuable learning opportunities. The aviation industry's evolution of crew resource management training exemplifies this approach: by studying how crew coordination influenced accident outcomes, the industry developed training that dramatically improved team performance during emergencies, contributing to a 71% reduction in crew-related accidents over three decades.

Continuous learning mechanisms distinguish resilient organizations. These include formal approaches like after-action reviews and incident analyses, along with informal practices that encourage sharing experiences across organizational boundaries. The nuclear power industry effectively facilitates this learning by disseminating detailed lessons from operational events throughout the industry, enabling broad organizational learning without requiring each facility to experience the same failures firsthand.

research. Traditional safety metrics focus on outcomes (accidents, incidents) or process compliance (procedure adherence), but these lag indicators provide limited insight into adaptive capacity. Leading indicators of resilience include recovery time after disruptions, the number of novel solutions developed during exercises, and the quality of adaptation to unexpected scenarios. Organizations that measure and develop these capabilities demonstrate enhanced performance during real-world disruptions.

The human element introduces both vulnerabilities and strengths to complex systems. Organizations that recognize this duality and design systems that mitigate human limitations while amplifying human adaptive capacities achieve true resilience. Rather than treating humans merely as components to be controlled, resilient systems harness uniquely human capabilities like creativity, adaptation, and collaborative problem-solving.

Technical solutions alone cannot achieve resilience in complex, dynamic environments. The most advanced technological systems still rely on human judgment during unprecedented situations. Organizations that invest in developing human capabilities through thoughtful system design, effective training, supportive organizational cultures, and continuous learning processes build the adaptive capacity essential for navigating an increasingly complex and unpredictable world. In this context, human factors represent not merely a challenge to be managed but a crucial resource to be cultivated in the pursuit of system resilience.

CHAPTER SEVEN

Monitoring and Feedback Loops

Monitoring and feedback loops represent one of the most fundamental mechanisms in both natural and designed systems. At their core, these systems involve the continuous observation of processes and conditions, followed by responsive adjustments to maintain or improve performance. Whether we examine biological homeostasis, engineering control systems, organizational learning, or personal development, the principles remain remarkably consistent: gather information, evaluate against desired states, implement adjustments, and repeat.

In today's complex and rapidly changing world, sophisticated monitoring and feedback mechanisms have become essential for survival and success across virtually every domain. From the micro-level of individual learning to the macro-level of global climate systems, understanding how to design and implement effective monitoring and feedback loops can mean the difference between thriving and failing.

The convergence of advanced sensor technologies, massive computational power, and sophisticated analytical techniques has transformed what's possible in monitoring and feedback systems. Organizations and individuals now have unprecedented capabilities to observe, analyze, and respond to changing conditions. However, this technological advancement brings its own challenges: information overload, signal-to-noise problems, and the need for increasingly nuanced interpretation frameworks. Modern feedback systems must navigate these complexities while maintaining the fundamental principles that make feedback effective.

The Anatomy of Effective Monitoring Systems

The foundation of any feedback loop begins with monitoring the systematic collection of relevant data. Effective monitoring systems share several essential characteristics regardless of their specific application. First, they must identify the critical variables that genuinely matter to system performance. In business, this might mean tracking key performance indicators rather than vanity metrics. In healthcare, it means monitoring vital signs that accurately reflect patient condition. The process of selecting what to monitor often represents the most consequential decision in system design, as it shapes everything that follows.

Second, monitoring must occur at appropriate frequencies. Some variables require continuous real-time tracking, while others might be meaningfully assessed at longer intervals. The sampling rate must match the rate of potential change in the system being monitored. Too frequently monitoring wastes resources and can create noise, while insufficient monitoring misses' critical information. In dynamic environments, adaptive sampling rates may prove most effective increasing frequency when conditions change rapidly and decreasing during periods of stability.

Third, effective monitoring incorporates multiple perspectives and data sources. Relying on a single metric or viewpoint often creates blind spots and vulnerabilities. The most robust monitoring systems triangulate information from diverse sources to create a comprehensive understanding of system state and performance. This multi-dimensional approach helps compensate for measurement errors or biases in any single data stream. In complex human systems like organizations, this might mean combining quantitative performance metrics with qualitative feedback, direct observation, and self-assessment tools.

Fourth, monitoring systems must balance breadth and depth. While comprehensive coverage provides security, excessive monitoring may result in information overload. The art is in striking the right balance between being comprehensive enough to capture key patterns and being focused enough to be actionable. This frequently involves a tiered approach, with ongoing monitoring of a core set of indicators supplemented by periodic deep dives into specific areas of interest or concern.

Finally, effective monitoring requires appropriate measurement techniques that capture true system behavior without distortion. The observer effect, where the act of measurement changes what's being measured, represents a significant challenge. Non-intrusive measurement techniques, proper calibration procedures, and awareness of measurement limitations all contribute to monitoring accuracy. In social systems, anonymous feedback mechanisms, observational techniques, and culture measurement tools help capture authentic information that might otherwise remain hidden.

From Data to Insight: Processing Monitoring Information

Raw data alone rarely provides value. The critical step between monitoring and response involves transforming data into meaningful insights. This process begins with filtering and organizing information to separate signal from noise. Statistical techniques like variance analysis, trend identification, and anomaly detection help identify meaningful patterns within data streams. More advanced approaches include machine learning algorithms that can recognize subtle patterns invisible to human observers and natural language processing systems that extract meaning from unstructured feedback.

Data validation represents an often overlooked but essential component of this process. Before analysis begins, monitoring data must be assessed for accuracy, completeness, and reliability. Validation procedures identify and address missing values, outliers, inconsistencies, and measurement errors. Sophisticated systems incorporate automated validation rules that flag problematic data for human review while allowing clean data to flow seamlessly into analysis pipelines.

Contextual interpretation represents the next crucial step. Data gains meaning only when evaluated against appropriate references, historical performance, industry benchmarks, or theoretical ideals. This comparative analysis transforms raw numbers into assessments of performance that can drive decision-making. For example, a manufacturing defect rate of 2% might seem acceptable until compared against an industry benchmark of 0.5% or the organization's historical performance of 1%. The art of contextual interpretation involves selecting relevant comparisons that illuminate meaningful insights rather than misleading contrasts.

The interpretation process must also account for interdependencies between variables. In complex systems, changes in one area often produce ripple effects elsewhere. Understanding these relationships allows for more sophisticated analysis that can identify root causes rather than merely symptoms. Network analysis, systems dynamics modeling, and causal inference techniques help map these interconnections and trace observed effects back to their origins. Without this system's perspective, organizations often find themselves treating symptoms while leaving underlying causes unaddressed.

Finally, the most advanced information processing systems incorporate predictive capabilities. Rather than merely describing current states, they use historical patterns and system dynamics to forecast future conditions, enabling proactive rather than reactive responses. Predictive models range from simple trend extrapolations to sophisticated machine learning algorithms that incorporate multiple variables and complex relationships. Scenario analysis and simulation techniques further enhance predictive power by exploring potential futures under different conditions and response strategies.

Designing Responsive Feedback Mechanisms

Once monitoring information has been processed into actionable insights, effective systems must translate these insights into appropriate responses. The design of these feedback mechanisms significantly influences system performance and adaptability.

The most basic distinction exists between negative and positive feedback. Negative feedback mechanisms work to counteract changes and maintain stability, like a thermostat adjusting heating to maintain a constant temperature. These homeostatic mechanisms prove essential in systems that require consistency and reliability. Positive feedback, conversely, amplifies changes, potentially creating virtuous or vicious cycles that transform systems. Innovation processes often leverage positive feedback to accelerate promising developments, while risk management systems watch for destructive positive feedback loops that could threaten system viability. Most complex systems require a balance of both types, stabilizing critical functions while allowing for growth and adaptation in others.

Response sensitivity represents another critical design consideration. Overly sensitive feedback creates oscillation and instability as the system overcompensates for minor variations. Insufficient sensitivity produces sluggish responses that fail to adequately address deviations. Well-designed systems incorporate appropriate thresholds and gradual response curves that match the needs of the specific context. Advanced control systems use proportional-integral-derivative (PID) controllers that respond not just to current deviations but to the rate of change and cumulative error over time. This sophisticated approach allows for responses calibrated to both immediate conditions and longer-term patterns.

Timing also plays a crucial role in feedback effectiveness. Delays between monitoring, decision-making, and implementation can significantly impair system performance. The most effective feedback mechanisms minimize these delays or account for them in their response calculations. When delays cannot be eliminated, as in many complex organizational processes, predictive models can compensate by initiating responses based on projected rather than current states. These forward-looking systems anticipate needs rather than merely reacting to them, overcoming inherent delays in response mechanisms.

Feedback mechanisms must also consider response capacity and resource constraints. Even perfectly designed feedback loops fail if the system lacks the resources or capabilities to implement necessary adjustments. Effective systems match response ambitions to available capacities and incorporate resource allocation mechanisms that prioritize the most critical adjustments when constraints prevent addressing all identified needs. This might involve triage processes in emergency services, priority matrices in project management, or constraint-based optimization in resource planning.

Finally, robust feedback systems incorporate multiple response options rather than rigid, binary reactions. This flexibility allows for proportional and contextually appropriate adjustments that can navigate complex situations more effectively than simplistic approaches. Decision trees, response protocols, and adaptive algorithms all provide structured approaches to matching specific conditions with appropriate responses. The most sophisticated systems learn from experience which responses work best in different situations, gradually refining their response selection processes over time.

Learning Systems: The Meta-Loop of Improvement

The most sophisticated monitoring and feedback systems incorporate not just one loop but multiple nested loops. Beyond responding to immediate conditions, these systems evaluate and improve their own performance over time creating what we might call meta-feedback loops or learning systems.

These learning systems monitor not just external variables but also their own monitoring accuracy, feedback effectiveness, and overall performance. They continuously refine what they measure, how they interpret information, and how they respond based on outcomes. This capacity for self-improvement represents a quantum leap in capability over static systems. While conventional feedback addresses current performance gaps, learning systems address systemic limitations in the feedback mechanisms themselves.

The architecture of learning systems typically involves primary operational loops that handle day-to-day adjustments, secondary evaluation loops that periodically assess effectiveness, and tertiary design loops that modify system structure based on accumulated learning. These nested timeframes allow the system to simultaneously maintain operational performance while evolving its fundamental capabilities. In organizations, this might manifest as daily performance adjustments, monthly process reviews, and annual strategic redesigns, each level informing the others through structured information flows.

Machine learning algorithms exemplify this approach, but learning systems exist in many domains. High-performing organizations implement after-action reviews to refine their processes. Effective teachers adjust their methods based on student outcomes. Even biological evolution represents a form of learning system operating across generations. The common thread across these diverse examples involves structured mechanisms for capturing experience, extracting patterns, and modifying future behavior accordingly.

The key to designing effective learning systems lies in creating clear mechanisms for evaluation and adaptation of the primary feedback loops. This requires metrics for assessing feedback effectiveness, processes for systematic review, and mechanisms for implementing structural improvements rather than merely operational adjustments. Knowledge management systems play a crucial role by capturing insights across instances and making them available for future iterations. Without these explicit learning mechanisms, systems may stumble upon improvements but cannot systematically advance their capabilities.

Implementation challenges for learning systems include maintaining operational stability while evolving capabilities, balancing exploration of new approaches with exploitation of proven methods and transferring insights across contexts without overgeneralizing. Successful learning systems navigate these tensions through phased implementation processes, controlled experimentation frameworks, and context-aware adaptation rules that modify general principles for specific situations.

Human Factors in Monitoring and Feedback

While technical aspects of monitoring and feedback design receive considerable attention, the human dimensions often prove equally critical to system success. Even the most sophisticated systems interact with human psychology, organizational dynamics, and social contexts in ways that profoundly influence outcomes.

Cognitive biases significantly affect how people interpret and respond to monitoring information. Confirmation bias leads people to overvalue data that supports existing beliefs. Recency bias overweight recent events compared to historical patterns. Attribution bias distorts assessments of causality, while availability bias skews risk perception based on memorable examples rather than true probabilities. Numerous other biases can distort perception and response if not consciously addressed through system design. Debiasing techniques include structured decision protocols, multiple independent assessments, and explicit recognition of common distortion patterns.

Emotional factors also play crucial roles. Fear of negative feedback can lead to avoidance or defensiveness. Performance monitoring often triggers anxiety that impairs functioning. Shame reactions can shut down learning rather than facilitating improvement. Well-designed systems account for these psychological realities and incorporate approaches that work with rather than against human nature. Psychological safety practices, growth mindset cultivation, and feedback techniques that preserve self-esteem all help overcome emotional barriers to effective feedback utilization.

Motivation and engagement represent another critical human dimension. Feedback systems designed without attention to motivational impacts often generate compliance rather than commitment. Effective approaches align feedback with intrinsic motivators like autonomy, mastery, and purpose rather than relying exclusively on extrinsic rewards and punishments. Gamification elements, progress visualization tools, and meaningful goal connections all enhance engagement with feedback processes. The most effective systems transform monitoring from an external imposition into a valued resource that helps people achieve their own objectives.

Group dynamics create additional complexities. Power differentials affect who receives attention in feedback discussions. Social pressure can silence critical perspectives. Cultural norms influence what kinds of feedback feel acceptable. Information silos prevent comprehensive system views. Effective systems build in mechanisms to mitigate these social distortions, such as anonymous input channels, facilitated cross-functional dialogues, and explicit norms that legitimize constructive criticism regardless of organizational position.

The most successful implementations recognize that monitoring and feedback systems exist within human contexts. They incorporate these human factors into design decisions rather than treating them as inconvenient aberrations from idealized technical models. This human-centered approach often means sacrificing some theoretical elegance for practical effectiveness, creating systems that work with real people rather than idealized rational actors.

Integrated Approaches: Unifying Technical and Social Dimensions

The most effective monitoring and feedback systems integrate technical excellence with human sensitivity, creating synergies rather than tradeoffs between these dimensions. This integration manifests in several key practices that bridge technical and social aspects of system design.

First, participatory design processes involve system users in creating monitoring and feedback mechanisms rather than imposing them from above. This participation increases both technical quality through incorporation of frontline knowledge and human acceptance, as people naturally support systems they helped create. Participatory approaches range from simple consultation to full co-creation methodologies where users shape fundamental system design. While these approaches require more time initially, they typically save resources later by avoiding resistance and retrofitting.

Second, integrated systems balance transparency with psychological safety. People need sufficient visibility in monitoring data to inform their decisions, but excessive transparency can create counterproductive pressure and anxiety. The most effective systems provide graduated access, comprehensive information for direct users, appropriate summaries for other stakeholders, and privacy protections that prevent misuse. Transparency also extends to the monitoring methods themselves, as understanding how data is collected and interpreted increases trust in the resulting feedback.

Third, integrated approaches emphasize learning rather than judgment. When monitoring becomes associated primarily with evaluation and consequences, it triggers defensive responses that undermine improvement. By explicitly separating development-focused feedback from evaluation processes, at least partially, organizations create psychological space for authentic engagement with performance information. This separation might involve different feedback channels, distinct timing for developmental versus evaluative discussions, or explicit messaging about feedback purpose.

Fourth, effective integration requires attention to feedback literacy and capabilities. Technical sophistication proves worthless if users lack the skills to interpret and apply the resulting information. Comprehensive systems include the development of these capabilities through training programs, coaching resources, and simplified tools that make feedback accessible to users with varying technical backgrounds. Just as user interfaces make complex computer systems accessible to non-programmers, well-designed feedback interfaces make sophisticated data meaningful to non-analysts.

Finally, truly integrated systems evolve their integration approaches themselves. They recognize that the appropriate balance of technical and human factors varies across contexts and time. Through systematic reflection and adaptation, these systems continually refine how they combine technical and social elements to maximize effectiveness in changing circumstances. This meta-adaptation represents the highest level of system sophistication, a self-aware process that evolves not just operational parameters but the fundamental approach to balancing competing design considerations.

CHAPTER EIGHT

Resilience Under Resource Constraints

Resilience under resource constraints represents one of humanity's most valuable adaptive capacities, the ability to not merely survive but genuinely thrive when faced with limitations. This seemingly paradoxical skill transcends mere endurance, encompassing our capacity to adapt, innovate, and flourish despite scarcity. Throughout human civilization, from ancient innovations born of necessity to modern breakthroughs emerging from crisis, history repeatedly demonstrates that constraint often serves as the mother of ingenuity. When resources are limited, whether financial capital, material goods, available time, skilled personnel, or natural resources, we are compelled to challenge our fundamental assumptions, sharpen our focus, and explore creative pathways that abundance might never have revealed. This constraint-driven innovation manifests across all scales of human experience: individuals finding personal growth through adversity, organizations discovering competitive advantages through efficiency, and entire societies developing cultural adaptations to environmental limitations. This chapter examines the multifaceted dimensions of resilience under resource constraints, offering insights into the psychological foundations, strategic approaches, social dynamics, and ethical frameworks that enable humans to transform perceived limitations into catalysts for unexpected growth, innovation, and sustainable prosperity.

The Paradox of Constraints: How Limitations Foster Creativity

The relationship between constraints and creativity represents one of the most counterintuitive yet well-documented phenomena in human psychology and organizational behavior. When resources flow abundantly, we instinctively gravitate toward solving problems through what might be called the "more approach," applying more money, more time, more people, or more materials until challenges yield. This approach, while occasionally effective, often bypasses the deeper cognitive processes that generate truly innovative solutions. Conversely, when resources become scarce, necessity activates different neural pathways, compelling us to question assumptions, challenge conventional approaches, and discover elegant solutions that might otherwise remain unexplored.

The historical record provides compelling evidence for this paradox. Consider how NASA engineers saved the Apollo 13 mission using only materials available on the damaged spacecraft, creating carbon dioxide scrubbers from space suits, duct tape, and plastic bags. Or how entrepreneurs like Steve Jobs and Steve Wozniak transformed technological limitations into design features, creating user-friendly computers when processing power was scarce. Even in artistic domains, constraints have produced masterpieces Ernest Hemingway's spare prose style developed partly from newspaper word count restrictions, while jazz improvisation evolved within the constraints of existing musical structures.

Contemporary research in cognitive psychology helps explain this phenomenon. When faced with obvious solutions enabled by abundant resources, our brains often engage in "satisficing," accepting the first adequate solution rather than searching for optimal ones. Constraints disrupt this tendency, activating deeper cognitive processes. Brain imaging studies show that when subjects face resource limitations while problem-solving, they exhibit increased activity in regions associated with divergent thinking and cognitive flexibility. These constraints force what psychologists call "lateral thinking," approaching problems from unexpected angles rather than following established patterns.

Organizations that deliberately introduce constraints often discover unexpected benefits. The practice of "timeboxing" in software development, strictly limiting development periods, frequently produces more elegant code than open-ended schedules. Similarly, companies imposing artificial budget constraints on innovation teams often report more creative outcomes than when providing unlimited funding. Even communication constraints, such as Twitter's character limits, have given rise to entirely new forms of expression and information transmission previously unimagined.

The key insight is that constraints provide essential structure to the creative process. Like riverbanks channeling water flow, constraints direct creative energy toward productive pathways rather than allowing it to dissipate across endless possibilities. By embracing constraints rather than merely tolerating them, individuals and organizations can transform limitations from obstacles into catalysts for breakthrough thinking.

Psychological Foundations of Resource Resilience

The capacity to thrive under resource constraints begins not with material assets but with psychological attributes that determine how we perceive and respond to limitation. Research across disciplines, from developmental psychology to organizational behavior, has identified several core psychological foundations that enable exceptional resilience amid scarcity.

Cognitive flexibility represents perhaps the most critical of these attributes: the ability to reframe challenges as opportunities and envision multiple pathways forward when conventional routes are blocked. This flexibility manifests what psychologists call "possibility thinking" rather than "necessity thinking." Those with high cognitive flexibility don't merely ask,

"How can we make do with what we have?" but rather, "What new possibilities might these constraints reveal?" This cognitive reorientation transforms the psychological experience of constraint from limitation to opportunity.

Equally important is an internal locus of control, the belief that one can influence outcomes despite external limitations. Those with a strong internal locus perceive resource constraints as challenges to overcome rather than immutable barriers. This orientation correlates strongly with proactive behavior, creative problem-solving, and persistence when facing obstacles. Conversely, those with an external locus often exhibit learned helplessness when confronting resource limitations, perceiving constraints as defining boundaries rather than starting points for innovation.

Tolerance for ambiguity and discomfort constitutes another crucial psychological foundation. Resource constraints inevitably create uncertainty about outcomes, timelines, and capabilities. Those who can function effectively amid this ambiguity maintain cognitive resources for problem-solving rather than expending mental energy on anxiety management. This tolerance connects to what psychologist's call "psychological hardiness," the capacity to remain committed, maintain control, and view challenges as growth opportunities even under stressful conditions.

The ability to distinguish between genuine necessities and perceived needs represents yet another psychological cornerstone of resource resilience. Those who thrive under constraints demonstrate remarkable clarity about priorities, readily distinguishing between essential requirements and habitual preferences. This discernment prevents resource depletion on non-critical activities while ensuring critical functions receive adequate support.

Crucially, research demonstrates that these psychological attributes can be systematically developed through intentional practice. Mindfulness techniques enhance cognitive flexibility by increasing awareness of automatic thought patterns and creating space for alternative perspectives. Cognitive reframing exercises deliberately identifying multiple interpretations of challenging situations and strengthen internal locus of control. Gradual exposure to increasingly difficult constraints builds tolerance for ambiguity while clarifying genuine priorities. Educational approaches that incorporate constraint-based challenges yield individuals better prepared for real-world resource limitations than those trained with abundant resources.

Organizations seeking to build resource resilience must therefore focus not merely on material resource management but on cultivating these psychological foundations across their workforce. Training programs, leadership modeling, and organizational culture all play vital roles in developing the collective psychological capacity to transform constraints into competitive advantages.

Strategic Minimalism: Doing More with Less

When resources become constrained, strategic minimalism emerges as a powerful methodology for maintaining effectiveness or even enhancing performance. Unlike simple cost-cutting or austerity measures, strategic minimalism represents a sophisticated approach to resource allocation based on maximizing impact while minimizing expenditure. This methodology encompasses several interconnected practices that transform resource limitations from liability to potential advantage.

The foundation of strategic minimalism begins with comprehensive resource assessment developing precise understanding of available assets across all categories: financial, material, human, temporal, informational, and relational. This assessment must move beyond obvious resources to identify hidden or underutilized assets. Organizations often discover significant "dark assets," resources invisible on balance sheets but valuable in operation, such as institutional knowledge, informal networks, or latent capabilities. Similarly, individuals conducting honest capability inventories frequently identify untapped skills or resources previously overlooked.

Following this assessment, ruthless prioritization becomes essential, identifying the vital few priorities that will yield maximum impact and deliberately eliminating or postponing everything else. This prioritization must transcend conventional cost-benefit analysis to incorporate impact-to-resource ratios that identify interventions generating disproportionate returns relative to investment. The Pareto Principle often applies roughly 20% of activities typically generate 80% of value. Strategic minimalism involves identifying that critical 20% and concentrating available resources accordingly.

Creative recombination represents another cornerstone of this approach, finding novel ways to leverage existing assets by reconfiguring or repurposing them for new applications. This might involve physical reconfiguration (repurposing infrastructure), temporal reconfiguration (restructuring schedules to maximize utilization), or capability recombination (creating cross-functional teams that leverage diverse skill sets). These recombination strategies frequently reveal resource capacity previously invisible within traditional operational frameworks.

Process simplification constitutes yet another strategic minimalist practice systematically eliminating unnecessary complexity that consumes resources without generating proportional value. This simplification requires challenging established procedures through first-principles thinking: "What is the essential outcome we need to achieve, and what is the simplest possible process for achieving it?" Organizations practicing this approach often discover that significant portions of their operations exist for historical rather than functional reasons, consuming resources that could be redirected toward higher-impact activities.

Perhaps counterintuitively, strategic minimalism sometimes involves strategic investment, allocating scarce resources toward capabilities that will significantly reduce future resource requirements. These investments typically focus on automation of repetitive processes, development of self-sustaining systems, or creation of force-multiplying tools that enhance productivity across multiple domains. While initially resource-intensive, these investments create what might be called "resource leverage," the ability to accomplish more with less over extended timeframes.

Organizations implementing strategic minimalism consistently discover that resource constraints often improve rather than diminish results by forcing clarity about priorities, eliminating distractions, reducing decision complexity, and focusing collective energy on critical outcomes. This insight applies equally across domains from corporate operations to nonprofit management to personal productivity to community development initiatives. In each case, the discipline imposed by resource constraints catalyzes a level of strategic thinking that abundance rarely inspires.

Social Capital: The Ultimate Renewable Resource

When material resources become severely constrained, social capital emerges as a powerful alternative resource, one that can compensate for material deficiencies while potentially expanding the effective resource base available to individuals and communities. Unlike physical resources, which typically follow rules of diminishing returns and depletion through use, social capital often exhibits opposite characteristics, increasing returns and growth through circulation.

Social capital encompasses the networks of relationships that enable collaboration, resource sharing, mutual support, and collective action. These networks function as informal insurance mechanisms during resource shortages, enabling communities to allocate limited resources more efficiently than market mechanisms alone could achieve. Historical examples abound, from traditional barn-raising practices in agricultural communities to modern mutual aid networks that emerge during economic downturns. Research consistently demonstrates that communities with robust social capital demonstrate significantly greater resilience during resource shocks than those with equivalent material resources but weaker social bonds.

The development of social capital depends on several interdependent factors. Trust forms the foundation of the confidence that cooperative behavior will be reciprocated rather than exploited. Communities with high trust levels can mobilize resources quickly during constraints, reallocating assets without excessive transaction costs or verification mechanisms. This trust develops through repeated positive interactions, transparent communication, and consistent fulfillment of commitments, particularly during challenging circumstances.

Reciprocity norms constitute another essential element: the shared understanding that assistance provided will eventually return to some form. These norms create "social credit systems" where individuals can draw on community resources during personal shortages with the expectation of contributing when their own resources recover. Unlike financial credit, these systems typically accommodate flexible repayment terms and recognition of diverse contribution forms, making them particularly valuable during systemic resource constraints when conventional credit mechanisms often fail.

Shared purpose represents a third critical component: collective agreement about priorities that enables coordinated resource allocation during constraints. Communities with clear shared purposes can rapidly mobilize limited resources toward agreed priorities without extensive negotiation or conflict. This coordination capacity becomes particularly valuable when constraints require difficult allocation decisions between competing needs.

Communication infrastructure, both technological and social, provides the essential connective tissue for social capital development. Regular information exchange about needs, resources, and opportunities enables efficient matching between those with specific capabilities and those requiring assistance. Modern digital platforms have dramatically expanded the potential scale of social capital networks, enabling resource sharing across previously insurmountable geographic and social boundaries.

Organizations and communities seeking to build resilience against resource constraints should therefore strategically invest in social capital development alongside conventional resource accumulation. This investment might include creating physical or virtual gathering spaces, establishing skill-sharing programs, developing resource exchange platforms, implementing cooperative ownership structures, or fostering cross-sector partnerships. Unlike material infrastructure, which typically depreciates over time, social infrastructure is often appreciated with use becoming stronger and more effective through regular activation.

The insight that social capital represents a renewable and potentially unlimited resource offers particular hope for communities facing persistent material constraints. By strategically shifting investment from material accumulation toward relationship development, such communities can potentially achieve greater effective resource capacity than would be possible through material acquisition alone.

Antifragility: Designing Systems That Thrive Under Stress

Beyond resilience, the ability to withstand disruption and return to equilibrium lies the more powerful concept of antifragility, introduced by scholar Nassim Nicholas Taleb to describe systems that actually improve under stress and constraint. This distinction proves crucial when designing systems intended to operate under persistent resource limitations. Resilient systems maintain functionality despite constraints; antifragile systems actually leverage constraints to become stronger, more adaptive, and more efficient.

Nature abounds with antifragile examples: immune systems that develop greater resistance through exposure to pathogens, muscles that strengthen through resistance training, brain neural networks that develop through challenge, and forest ecosystems that depend on occasional fires for renewal and biodiversity. These natural systems don't merely tolerate stress; they require it for optimal development and evolution. Human-designed systems can similarly incorporate principles that transform resource constraints from threats into developmental catalysts.

Achieving antifragility under resource constraints begins with embracing variability rather than attempting to eliminate it. Traditional resource management often prioritizes stability and predictability, seeking to minimize fluctuations through buffers and reserves. While this approach provides short-term protection, it often creates long-term fragility by preventing adaptive responses to changing conditions. Antifragile systems instead incorporate deliberate variability, fluctuating resource allocations, rotating constraints, and periodic stress testing that triggers continuous adaptation and improvement.

Redundancy in critical functions, maintaining multiple pathways for achieving essential outcomes, represents another antifragility principle particularly relevant under resource constraints. Unlike efficiency-focused systems that eliminate redundancy to reduce costs, antifragile systems preserve redundancy in vital functions while accepting constraints in non-essential areas. This strategic redundancy creates what ecologists call "response diversity," multiple mechanisms for maintaining critical functionality when primary approaches fail.

Decentralization of authority and decision-making constitutes a third antifragility element. Centralized command structures, while appearing efficient, often create fragility under resource constraints by developing information bottlenecks and response delays. Distributed authority systems where decision-making occurs close to implementation typically demonstrate greater adaptive capacity when resources suddenly become limited. This decentralization allows rapid local optimization without waiting for system-wide coordination.

Iterative learning processes and systematic mechanisms for extracting information from failures and successes provide another essential antifragility component. Such processes transform constraints and disruptions from mere obstacles into valuable data sources that inform system evolution. Organizations implementing robust after-action reviews, blameless post-mortems, and rapid experimentation cycles regularly outperform competitors under resource constraints despite sometimes appearing less efficient during stable periods.

Appropriate feedback mechanisms that rapidly communicate system states across components complete the antifragility framework. These mechanisms enable coordinated adaptation to changing resource conditions without centralized control. Natural systems utilize chemical signals, neural impulses, and environmental cues for this purpose; human organizations can develop analogous information flows through transparent metrics, rapid communication channels, and intuitive visualization tools.

When designing organizations, communities, or personal practices under resource constraints, the goal shouldn't be merely efficiency, which often creates fragility through the elimination of margins, but rather developing these antifragile properties that transform stress into strength. By embracing variability, maintaining strategic redundancy, decentralizing authority, implementing iterative learning, and establishing effective feedback mechanisms, we can create entities that actually benefit from the very constraints that would cripple more rigid structures.

The Ethical Dimensions of Scarcity and Abundance

Resource constraints inevitably raise profound ethical questions that transcend technical considerations of efficiency or optimization. When not everyone can have everything, fundamental questions emerge: How should limited resources be distributed? Who should decide allocation priorities? What values should guide these decisions? What obligations exist between those with more and those with less? These questions apply across scales from personal budgeting decisions to global resource distribution challenges and their answers reveal deeply held values about justice, community, and human flourishing.

Traditional economic approaches to resource allocation typically emphasize maximizing efficiency by directing resources toward their highest-valued uses as determined by market mechanisms. While powerful, this approach often fails to address distributive justice concerns, particularly when initial resource endowments reflect historical inequities rather than legitimate differences in contribution or need. It also frequently undervalues common resources and non-monetized goods like ecosystem services, community cohesion, or cultural heritage.

Alternative ethical frameworks offer different perspectives on navigating resource constraints. Utilitarian approaches seek the greatest good for the greatest number, sometimes justifying significant inequalities if they produce greater aggregate welfare. Rights-based approaches emphasize minimum thresholds of resource access necessary for human dignity and capability development, regardless of efficiency impacts. Virtue ethics traditions focus on developing attitudes toward resources neither grasping attachment nor careless waste that foster individual character and community flourishing.

Indigenous and traditional cultures worldwide have developed sophisticated ethical systems for managing shared resources sustainably over generations. These systems typically emphasize stewardship over ownership, sufficiency over excess, and intergenerational responsibility over short-term maximization. The ancient Hawaiian ahupuaʻa system, for instance, managed resources from mountain watersheds to ocean fisheries through complex ethical codes governing harvesting practices, sharing obligations, and conservation requirements. Similar systems exist across cultures, offering valuable wisdom relevant to contemporary resource challenges.

Too often, perceived scarcity triggers fear-based responses, hoarding behaviors, exploitation of vulnerabilities, and zero-sum competitive thinking that ultimately diminish collective resilience. These reactions, while psychologically understandable, frequently create artificial scarcity by disrupting distribution systems, undermining trust, and preventing cooperative solutions that could expand the effective resource base. The resulting spiral of distrust and competition often depletes resources faster than the original constraint would have required.

Alternative ethical responses emphasize what might be called "conscious constraint," deliberately limiting consumption below capacity in recognition of broader systemic impacts and future needs. This approach acknowledges that true abundance comes not from accumulating resources beyond need but from creating systems where resources flow efficiently to where they generate the greatest benefit. Such ethical frameworks recognize the distinction between material simplicity (limiting resource consumption) and life simplicity (reducing complexity and distraction), the former potentially enhancing the latter rather than diminishing it.

Organizations and communities navigating resource constraints benefit from explicitly addressing these ethical dimensions rather than treating allocation as purely technical problems. Transparent processes for determining priorities, clear articulation of values guiding decisions, and mechanisms for ensuring equitable voice in deliberations all contribute to maintaining social cohesion during constraint periods. Without this ethical foundation, technically sound resource management approaches often fail through lack of legitimacy and subsequent non-compliance.

By consciously developing ethical frameworks appropriate to their contexts, individuals and organizations can transform resource constraints from sources of conflict into opportunities for deepening shared values and strengthening community bonds. These frameworks enable the development of more resilient approaches to resource constraints approaches that strengthen rather than fragment communities, that regenerate rather than deplete common resources, and that distribute both burdens and benefits in ways that enhance collective flourishing even amid material limitations.

CHAPTER NINE

Antifragility Systems That Gain From Disorder

Antifragility represents a profound paradigm shift in how we understand systems and their relationship with uncertainty. First formalized and named by risk analyst and philosopher Nassim Nicholas Taleb, the concept identifies a property that exists beyond mere robustness or resilience. Unlike fragile systems that break under pressure or merely robust ones that withstand stress unchanged, antifragile systems actually improve, strengthen, and evolve when exposed to volatility, randomness, and disorder. This concept transcends traditional notions of resilience by suggesting that certain forms of volatility aren't merely to be endured but actively sought out as catalysts for growth.

Antifragility exists on a spectrum: fragile-robust-antifragile, where each position represents fundamentally different responses to stressors. Fragile systems suffer from volatility, like fine China breaking under stress or a highly leveraged investment portfolio collapsing during market turbulence. Robust systems remain unchanged by volatility, like a reinforced concrete wall standing firm against storms or a diversified portfolio maintaining stable value through market fluctuations. Antifragile systems, however, benefit from volatility, like immune systems becoming stronger after pathogen exposure or entrepreneurial ventures discovering new opportunities during market disruptions.

Natural systems have evolved antifragile properties through millions of years of evolutionary pressure. Ecological diversity increases resilience to environmental changes forests with varied species better withstand disease outbreaks than monocultures. The human body strengthens in response to appropriate stressors, from muscle development to immune function. Biological systems typically feature redundancy rather than efficiency. We have two kidneys, excess capacity in our lungs, and multiple pathways for critical biological processes. This seemingly "wasteful" design creates capacity for adaptation under stress that purely efficient systems lack.

In stark contrast, most modern human-designed systems prioritize efficiency over antifragility. Just-in-time manufacturing creates fragility to supply chain disruptions by eliminating inventory buffers. Cost-cutting initiatives often eliminate redundancy that provides essential safety margins during crises. Bureaucratic centralization reduces system adaptability by slowing response times and creating single points of failure. The ruthless pursuit of optimization and efficiency has created hidden vulnerabilities throughout our technological, economic, and organizational systems.

The concept fundamentally inverts traditional risk management approaches. Rather than attempting to predict and avoid rare events, an impossible task in complex systems, antifragility embraces controlled exposure to volatility. This perspective suggests that suppressing normal volatility patterns actually increases systemic risk by preventing small, beneficial corrections from occurring naturally. When systems never encounter minor stressors, they lose the ability to adapt and respond appropriately when major challenges inevitably arrive.

Antifragility challenges the modernist notion that control, and predictability should be our primary goals when designing systems. Instead, it suggests that variation, randomness, and certain forms of stress are not just inevitable but necessary components of healthy, evolving systems. This represents a fundamental reorientation in design philosophy that reaches across disciplines from personal health to international economics.

Hormesis: How Stress Creates Strength

The biological principle of hormesis provides a perfect illustration of antifragility at work. When organisms experience moderate stressors or carefully calibrated amounts of challenge or adversity, they respond by becoming stronger, more adaptable, and more capable of handling future threats. This adaptive response mechanism reveals how antifragility manifests across diverse domains of life and offers powerful insights into designing systems that thrive under pressure.

Exercise damages muscle tissue through microtears, which then rebuilds stronger than before. Progressive overload in strength training exemplifies this principle: gradually increasing resistance forces muscular adaptation. The body responds to physical demands by increasing bone density, improving cardiovascular capacity, enhancing mitochondrial function, and optimizing neurological recruitment of muscle fibers. Without this stress-induced adaptation, physical capabilities deteriorate through disuse atrophy. The body allocates resources based on demonstrated need rather than maintaining unused capacities.

Similarly, the immune system develops robustness through exposure to pathogens. Vaccination works precisely because controlled exposure to weakened pathogens triggers immune memory without overwhelming the body's defenses. Children raised in excessively sterile environments often develop compromised immune function and allergies, as the system never learns appropriate response calibration. The "hygiene hypothesis" suggests that modern increases in autoimmune disorders partially stem from insufficient immune system training through environmental exposure.

Heat and cold exposure through saunas, cold plunges, or environmental variation stimulate physiological adaptations that improve cardiovascular function and stress resistance. Temperature challenges trigger heat shock proteins that repair cellular damage and improve resistance to various stressors. Cold exposure increases metabolic efficiency and activates brown fat thermogenesis. These traditional practices, found across diverse cultures, harness hormetic responses to improve physiological resilience.

Even certain toxins in small doses can trigger beneficial physiological responses, while the same substances in large quantities would prove harmful. Plant phytochemicals often function this way mildly toxic to pests but are beneficial to humans in appropriate doses. Substances like curcumin, resveratrol, and sulforaphane create mild cellular stress that activates defense mechanisms and antioxidant production. These compounds, present in traditional food plants, exemplify how mild chemical stressors can improve long-term health outcomes.

This principle extends beyond physical domains into psychological and intellectual realms. Cognitive challenges and problem-solving build mental capacity through neuroplasticity. Children sheltered from all frustration fail to develop emotional resilience necessary for adulthood. Learning occurs most effectively in the "productive struggle" zone not so easy as to be boring, not so difficult as to cause despair. The brain, like muscles, develops in response to appropriate challenge rather than comfort.

Hormesis applies to social systems as well. Communities that occasionally face moderate hardship often develop stronger social bonds and cooperative mechanisms than those never tested. Organizations experiencing controlled challenges develop adaptive capabilities and internal cohesion. Even economies benefit from small recessions that clear inefficient enterprises and reallocate resources toward more productive uses. The suppression of these corrective mechanisms often leads to larger, more devastating crises when accumulated tensions eventually break through.

The critical insight from hormesis is the non-linear response curve small doses of stressors produce benefits, while excessive amounts cause harm. The art of creating antifragile systems lies in finding this optimal range where stress induces adaptation without overwhelming capacity to respond. This principle suggests that completely eliminating stressors from natural systems often proves counterproductive, as certain forms of adversity drive beneficial adaptation.

Economic Systems: Fragility Through Intervention

Modern economic systems often sacrifice antifragility in pursuit of short-term stability. By dampening volatility through excessive intervention, we create increasingly fragile structures that become vulnerable to catastrophic failure. The illusion of control in complex economic systems generates hidden vulnerabilities that manifest unexpectedly during crisis events, often with devastating consequences that far outweigh the benefits of temporarily suppressed volatility.

Natural systems demonstrate the danger of suppressing normal volatility cycles. In forest management, preventing small, regular fires allows the underbrush to accumulate, eventually fueling devastating megafires no system can withstand. This pattern repeats across domains small, frequent disturbances clear vulnerabilities before they accumulate into system-threatening proportions. Economic systems follow similar patterns, where preventing normal market corrections allows structural imbalances to grow unchecked.

The boom-bust cycle represents a natural correction mechanism in market economies. During downturns, inefficient firms fail, overleveraged investments unwind, and resources reallocate toward more productive uses. While painful in the short term, these processes maintain long-term system health by clearing malinvestment. When central banks and governments intervene aggressively to prevent all downturns, they interrupt this corrective mechanism, allowing deeper systemic vulnerabilities to accumulate.

Financial engineering often creates an appearance of stability while masking increasing fragility. Complex derivatives and leverage can generate steady returns during normal periods while concealing catastrophic tail risks. This pattern manifested dramatically during the 2008 financial crisis, when mortgage-backed securities rated as ultra-safe suddenly revealed catastrophic vulnerabilities. The mathematical models underlying these instruments failed to account for correlated risks and black swan events, creating an illusion of safety that encouraged excessive risk-taking throughout the system.

Centralized economic planning eliminates the beneficial bottom-up adaptation that occurs through market processes and distributed decision-making. When economic decisions concentrate in the hands of a few policymakers, the system loses access to the distributed intelligence and local knowledge embedded in millions of independent decision-makers. This concentration creates brittleness. When central planners err, the entire system suffers simultaneously rather than experiencing limited, contained failures that provide information without systemic collapse.

The banking system illustrates these principles clearly. When structured with insufficient reserves and excessive interconnection, attempts to eliminate all bank failures through regulation and intervention paradoxically increase the likelihood of systemic collapse. Traditional banking recognized this risk through higher capital requirements and clearer separation between different types of financial activities. Modern financial innovation has created unprecedented interconnection, where the failure of one institution threatens the entire global system the very definition of fragility.

Government debt demonstrates similar dynamics, providing short-term benefits while potentially creating long-term vulnerabilities. Nations that consistently run deficits during good times lack the fiscal capacity to respond during genuine emergencies. The appearance of stability often masks accumulating fragilities beneath the surface. Countries maintaining fiscal discipline through economic cycles retain policy flexibility during crises an antifragile position that benefits from volatility by creating optionality when others face constraints.

Price controls and market interventions often backfire by preventing natural price discovery processes. When prices cannot adjust freely to reflect changing conditions, resources misallocate, and shortages develop. Housing markets demonstrate this principle when rent control policies reduce housing supply and quality over time. Energy markets show similar patterns when price caps prevent appropriate conservation responses during scarcity. The attempt to eliminate price volatility creates structural distortions that eventually require more painful adjustments.

The concept of moral hazard pervades fragile economic systems. When market participants believe they'll be protected from downside risks through bailouts or interventions, they take excessive risks that endanger the entire system. The "Greenspan put," the market belief that the Federal

Reserve would intervene to prevent significant market declines, exemplifies this dynamic. Such implicit guarantees encourage reckless behavior while socializing losses, creating fundamental asymmetries that undermine system stability.

True economic antifragility would embrace certain forms of volatility rather than attempting to eliminate them. This might include allowing firms to fail, permitting interest rates to reflect market conditions rather than policy objectives, maintaining counter-cyclical fiscal policies, and designing financial regulations that prioritize system resilience over short-term growth metrics. These approaches would likely produce more frequent small adjustments but fewer catastrophic crises, the hallmark of an antifragile system.

The Barbell Strategy: Practical Antifragility

The barbell strategy represents a practical approach to implementing antifragility in decision-making across domains. By combining extreme risk aversion on one end with calculated risk-taking on the other while avoiding the middle, individuals and organizations can position themselves to both survive shocks and benefit from upside volatility. This asymmetric positioning creates exposure to positive Black Swan events while limiting downside risk, embodying antifragility's core principle of gaining from disorder.

In investment, this means keeping the majority of assets extremely safe while allocating a small portion to high-risk, high-reward opportunities. Rather than a "diversified" moderate-risk portfolio distributed along a normal curve, the barbell approach might combine treasury bonds or physical precious metals with venture capital investments or options strategies, creating asymmetric exposure to upside volatility. This structure ensures survival through worst-case scenarios while maintaining exposure to exponential growth opportunities.

The strategy relies heavily on optionality arrangements with limited downside risk but unlimited upside potential. Stock options exemplify this structure, as do certain career paths that combine stable employment with entrepreneurial ventures. Book authors demonstrate this pattern when they maintain day jobs while writing, limiting downside while creating exposure to bestseller possibilities. Venture capital follows similar principles by making many small investments with capped losses but unlimited upside potential in the few that succeed dramatically.

From a life planning perspective, the barbell strategy might mean maintaining practical skills for stable income while exploring creative pursuits with potentially exponential rewards. Rather than pursuing a "balanced" middle path, this approach embraces extremes, becoming highly skilled in established domains while simultaneously exploring experimental territories. This creates both security and opportunity, rather than the mediocrity that often results from moderate approaches to all decisions.

The barbell approach balances tradition with innovation. Time-tested wisdom provides a foundation of reliability, while controlled experimentation enables discovery and adaptation. In dietary terms, this means emphasizing foods humans have consumed for millennia while remaining open to evidence-based nutritional discoveries. In education, it suggests mastering fundamental disciplines while exploring interdisciplinary connections. In organizational design, it means maintaining core processes that work reliably while encouraging innovative experiments at the margins.

Redundancy plays a crucial role in the barbell strategy. Multiple income streams, energy sources, or supply chains create resilience against disruption. The apparent "inefficiency" of redundancy actually creates antifragility by distributing risk and providing backup systems during stress events. The short-term costs of maintaining excess capacity are insurance against catastrophic failure. Nature consistently employs redundancy, from duplicate organs to diverse species fulfilling similar ecological niches, as protection against unexpected challenges.

Geographic diversification represents another form of the barbell strategy. Maintaining connections to multiple locations provides optionality during regional disruptions, whether economic, political, or environmental. This might involve dividing investments across jurisdictions, maintaining dual citizenship options, or developing the capacity to operate businesses remotely. During the COVID-19 pandemic, those with geographic flexibility could relocate to areas with better conditions for their needs, providing a clear antifragile advantage during systemic stress.

In terms of personal skill development, the barbell strategy recommends developing deep expertise in foundational skills while maintaining breadth across domains. Rather than becoming a pure specialist or pure generalist, this approach develops T-shaped knowledge depth in key areas while also fostering connective understanding between disciplines. This structure offers both specialized value and adaptability when conditions change unexpectedly.

The barbell strategy is fundamentally based on asymmetry, seeking arrangements in which potential gains far outweigh potential losses. This principle applies to a variety of domains, including financial investments and personal relationships. By systematically limiting downside exposure while maintaining unlimited upside potential, practitioners of the barbell strategy position themselves to benefit disproportionately from volatility, altering the definition of antifragility.

Beyond Prediction: Designing for Unknown Unknowns

Perhaps the most powerful application of antifragility is navigating a world of fundamental uncertainty. Instead of attempting to forecast unpredictable events, we can create systems that thrive in the face of uncertainty. This represents a significant philosophical shift in how we approach complexity and planning, from brittle prediction-based models to adaptive systems that benefit from randomness and surprise.

Traditional forecasting focuses on predicting specific outcomes, which is an inherently fragile approach in complex systems. Antifragile design, on the other hand, emphasizes resilience to prediction errors. The question has changed from "What will happen?" to "How will our system perform regardless of what happens?" This approach acknowledges the limitations of human foresight and embraces radical uncertainty as an inescapable feature of complex systems. Rather than building elaborate prediction models, antifragile systems prepare for wide outcome distributions.

Decentralization creates antifragility through distributed decision-making. When authority and capability reside closer to information sources, systems can respond adaptively to changing conditions. This contrasts with brittle, centralized structures that result in single points of failure and slow response times. Nature consistently uses decentralized designs, such as ant colonies and neural networks, to create adaptable, anti-fragile systems. Human organizations also benefit from subsidiarity, which pushes decisions to the lowest practical level with the highest information quality.

Experimentation and tinkering enable evolutionary mechanisms for system improvement. Rather than implementing comprehensive top-down designs, antifragile systems evolve through trial-and-error processes that identify improvements while containing failures. This "stochastic tinkering" harnesses randomness as a creative force, allowing beneficial variations to emerge organically. Silicon Valley's startup ecosystem exemplifies this approach: many small experiments yield occasional breakthrough innovations that compensate for numerous failures.

Small, frequent failures serve as information-gathering mechanisms that prevent catastrophe. When systems break in small ways, they reveal vulnerabilities before those weaknesses can accumulate into systemic failure. Organizations that punish all failure create fragility by driving problems underground, while those that permit certain types of controlled failure create evolutionary learning mechanisms. A "fail fast, fail small" approach creates antifragility by converting failures into valuable information while limiting their impact.

Via negative, or improvement through removal rather than addition, provides another anti-fragile strategy for handling uncertainty. Often, removing harmful elements results in better outcomes than adding new interventions. In medicine, this could entail discontinuing unnecessary medications. In product design, it entails removing unnecessary features. In governance, it suggests repealing harmful regulations rather than enacting compensatory measures. This subtractive approach recognizes the possibility of unintended consequences from complex interventions in systems that we do not fully understand.

Skin in the game Aligning decision-making authority with consequence exposure promotes natural antifragility in social systems. When decision-makers personally bear the costs of their errors, they naturally develop more prudent, reality-tested approaches. Conversely, systems allowing consequence transfer to create moral hazard and accumulating risk. Industries where key actors bear limited personal liability for catastrophic failures, like banking or certain types of corporate management systematically accumulates hidden risks that eventually manifest as system-wide crises.

Optionality provides perhaps the most powerful antifragile strategy for navigating uncertainty. By maintaining multiple possible paths forward without committing prematurely, systems preserve adaptive capacity regardless of which scenario unfolds. Financial options exemplify this principle, but optionality extends far beyond finance into education, career planning, technology adoption, and organizational design. The capacity to pursue multiple possibilities simultaneously and then double down on what works creates systems that benefit from unpredictability rather than suffering from it.

The concept of antifragility ultimately offers a radically different lens through which to view risk and uncertainty in a complex world. By recognizing that certain forms of disorder, volatility, and stress are not merely necessary evils but potential sources of growth and improvement, we open ourselves to more sustainable and adaptive approaches to building systems whether in business, government, technology, or our personal lives. The anti-fragile mindset celebrates the randomness inherent in complex systems rather than futilely attempting to eliminate it, transforming uncertainty from enemy to ally.

Antifragility is more than just an abstract concept; it is a practical design principle for navigating an increasingly complex and uncertain world. By incorporating these principles into our systems, ranging from personal health regimens to global financial structures, we can create entities that not only survive but also benefit from volatility. This transition from fragility to robustness to antifragility may be critical as we confront unprecedented levels of complexity, interconnection, and change in the coming decades. The systems that thrive will be those that are designed to benefit from the inevitable surprises of the future rather than predict it perfectly.

CHAPTER TEN

Resilience as a process continuous refactoring in changing environments

In a world full of constant change and uncertainty, resilience emerges not as a static trait but as a dynamic process of adaptation and growth. This chapter explores how resilience functions as an ongoing practice of continuous refactoring, the deliberate restructuring of our approaches, mindsets, and systems in response to changing environments. By understanding resilience as a process rather than an endpoint, we can develop more sustainable and adaptive strategies for navigating complexity. The metaphor of refactoring, borrowed from software development, aptly captures this iterative improvement process: systematically restructuring existing elements without changing external functionality but enhancing internal adaptability and performance under stress.

Resilience begins with recognizing the natural cycles of disruption and reorganization that characterize all complex systems. Just as forests require periodic fires to clear the underbrush and stimulate new growth, human systems benefit from moments of creative destruction. The adaptive cycle involves four distinct phases: exploitation (rapid growth), conservation (stability and efficiency), release (disruption), and reorganization (innovation).

In the exploitation phase, resources are readily available, and systems expand rapidly. This period is marked by entrepreneurial energy, quick learning, and flexible structures. Organizations in this phase prioritize exploration over efficiency, investing in diverse approaches and accepting higher failure rates as the cost of innovation. Individual resilience during this phase often manifests as curiosity, risk-taking, and rapid skill acquisition.

The conservation phase follows as systems mature, becoming increasingly efficient but also more rigid. Resources become locked into specialized functions, and emphasis shifts to optimization and standardization. While this creates short-term stability, it often reduces adaptive capacity. During this phase, resilient entities maintain awareness of the trade-off between efficiency and adaptability, deliberately preserving some redundancy and slack resources.

The release phase occurs when external shocks or internal contradictions trigger systemic breakdown. What seemed like stable structures suddenly collapsed, releasing previously bound resources. Though often experienced as a crisis, this creative destruction clears space for renewal. Resilient individuals and organizations distinguish themselves during this phase by accepting the inevitability of disruption, maintaining emotional regulation during turmoil, and rapidly identifying which elements to preserve and which to release.

Finally, the reorganization phase represents the critical window where novel configurations emerge. Here, experimentation and recombination of elements create new possibilities. This phase requires tolerance for ambiguity and the ability to operate effectively in undefined spaces. Rather than rushing to recreate previous structures, resilient systems use this period to test multiple alternatives before committing to new pathways.

By understanding where they are in this cycle, individuals and organizations can better calibrate their responses, knowing when to invest in growth, when to consolidate gains, when to let go of unsustainable patterns, and when to experiment with novel approaches. The most resilient entities develop the capacity to navigate all four phases skillfully, recognizing that each serves essential functions in the larger process of adaptation.

Antifragility: Gaining from Disorder

Resilience as a process moves beyond mere robustness to embrace what philosopher Nassim Taleb calls "antifragility," the capacity to actually benefit from stressors, volatility, and disorder. Unlike fragile systems that break under pressure or robust systems that merely withstand it, antifragile systems grow stronger through appropriate exposure to challenges.

This antifragile quality manifests at multiple levels. Biologically, it appears in hormesis, the phenomenon where low-dose exposure to stressors triggers beneficial adaptive responses. Examples include exercise (which stresses muscles and cardiovascular systems in ways that strengthen them) and immune function (where controlled exposure to pathogens builds resistance). Cognitively, it emerges when we encounter and resolve contradictions in our thinking, developing more nuanced mental models. Socially, it occurs when groups face and successfully navigate conflicts, emerging with stronger norms and deeper trust.

Cultivating antifragility requires several key practices. First is the principle of via negative, improvement through subtraction rather than addition. By systematically eliminating fragilities and dependencies, systems become less vulnerable to disruption. This might involve reducing debt, simplifying processes, or eliminating single points of failure.

Second is the deliberate introduction of hermetic stressors challenges substantial enough to trigger adaptation but not so overwhelming as to cause collapse. Organizations implement this through controlled experimentation, regular "pre-mortems" that anticipate failure modes, and simulations of potential disruptions. Individuals practice it through deliberate discomfort, stretching assignments, and measured risk-taking.

Third is the development of optionality, maintaining multiple possible paths forward rather than committing to singular strategies. This manifests as modular design in technical systems, career versatility in individuals, and strategic flexibility in organizations. By preserving options, systems can rapidly pivot when conditions change.

Fourth is the barbell strategy, combining conservative approaches in core areas with calculated risk-taking in limited domains. This might mean maintaining strong cash reserves while investing small amounts in high-risk, high-reward opportunities or preserving proven methods while experimenting with radical innovations in contained environments.

The goal is not to eliminate all stressors but to engage with them selectively and strategically, transforming potential threats into catalysts for development. This requires distinguishing between productive stressors that build capacity and destructive ones that deplete it, a discernment that develops through reflective experience and systems thinking.

Psychological Flexibility: The Internal Dimension

The process of resilience requires not only external adaptation but also internal refactoring, the continuous reworking of our mental models, emotional responses, and core narratives. Psychological flexibility represents our capacity to hold our perspectives lightly, making room for contradictory information and evolving our understanding as new data emerges.

This flexibility operates across several domains. Cognitive flexibility involves the ability to shift between different conceptual frameworks, considering multiple perspectives and reframing challenges. When faced with setbacks, psychologically flexible individuals can transform threats into challenges, obstacles into opportunities, and failures into learning experiences. This cognitive reappraisal process involves deliberately examining interpretations, challenging limiting assumptions, and constructing more empowering narratives without denying reality.

Emotional flexibility involves the capacity to experience the full range of emotions without being overwhelmed or controlled by them. This requires developing emotional granularity, the ability to distinguish between subtle emotional states, and emotional regulation strategies that neither suppress feelings nor amplify them unnecessarily. Practices such as mindfulness meditation enhance this flexibility by creating space between emotional triggers and responses, allowing for more considered reactions.

Behavioral flexibility manifests as "response breadth," an expanded repertoire of possible actions in challenging situations. Where rigid individuals have limited behavioral options (fight, flight, freeze), flexible individuals can access a wider range of responses calibrated to specific contexts. This behavioral agility allows for adaptive persistence, knowing when to maintain course despite obstacles and when to pivot to alternative approaches.

Identity flexibility involves holding self-concepts that can evolve without threatening core values. Rather than defining themselves by fixed traits or roles, resilient individuals construct narrative identities organized around themes of growth and transformation. They integrate failures and successes alike into coherent but evolving self-stories that accommodate change without losing continuity.

Developing psychological flexibility requires specific practices. These include perspective-taking exercises that challenge us to understand opposing viewpoints, mindfulness practices that create awareness of automatic reactions, exposure to constructive discomfort that stretches comfort zones, and reflective routines that help process experiences into learning. Through these practices, individuals develop not just greater tolerance for ambiguity but actual comfort with uncertainty, recognizing it as the space where growth occurs.

Distributed Resilience: The Network Effect

Resilience is rarely an individual achievement but rather emerges through connections and collaborations. The most enduring form of continuous refactoring happens at the network level, where diverse relationships and cross-boundary exchanges enhance adaptive capacity through complementary strengths and distributed intelligence.

Network resilience operates through several key mechanisms. Resource diversity ensures systems have access to varied skills, knowledge, and support when challenges arise. No single node possesses all necessary resources, but the network collectively maintains redundant capacities that can be mobilized as needed. This distributed redundancy provides insurance against localized failures without sacrificing overall efficiency.

Information diversity accelerates adaptation by exposing network members to varied perspectives and data sources. When information flows freely across boundaries between dissimilar groups (bridging social capital), novel insights emerge that can't arise within homogeneous clusters. These "weak tie" connections to different social worlds introduce potentially transformative ideas that help systems anticipate and adapt to emerging challenges.

Response diversity, or different ways of responding to similar stimuli, gives networks an experimental advantage. When facing novel challenges, networks with varied response patterns can test multiple approaches simultaneously, quickly identifying which strategies work best under current conditions. This parallel processing accelerates adaptation compared to hierarchical systems that must be committed to singular approaches.

Modularity allows portions of networks to fail without collapsing entire systems. When connections between components are strategically arranged, tightly coupled within modules but loosely coupled between them, disruptions remain contained rather than cascading. This balance between integration and separation creates systems that are both efficient during stable periods and resilient during disruption.

Cultivating network resilience requires deliberate practices. These include establishing psychological safety that encourages authentic exchange of ideas and concerns, developing boundary-spanning roles that connect different domains, creating regular forums for cross-functional collaboration, and establishing rapid feedback mechanisms that accelerate collective learning. Organizations enhance distributed resilience by mapping their informal networks, identifying potential vulnerabilities (such as overreliance on key individuals), and strategically building connections that enhance overall system adaptability.

The most resilient networks maintain productive tension between stability and change, with some relationships providing consistent support and others challenging comfortable assumptions. By developing what network theorists call "ambidexterity," the capacity to simultaneously exploit existing knowledge while exploring new possibilities, these networks continuously refactor themselves in response to changing environments.

Resilience Literacy: Learning to Read Change

Ultimately, resilience as a process requires developing what might be called "resilience literacy," the ability to read patterns of change, identify leverage points, and respond with appropriate strategies. This literacy represents a meta-capacity that enables continuous learning about how systems respond to disruption.

Resilience literacy begins with pattern recognition, the ability to distinguish between different types of challenges and their signature characteristics. Acute shocks require different responses than chronic strains; technical problems need different approaches than adaptive challenges; linear, predictable changes demand different strategies than complex, emergent ones. By developing taxonomies of change, individuals and organizations can more quickly categorize emerging situations and access relevant response repertoires.

Temporal literacy, or understanding how changes unfold over different time horizons, is another critical component. Resilient entities develop the capacity to simultaneously operate on multiple timescales, addressing immediate pressures while investing in long-term adaptability. They recognize both fast variables (those that change quickly and visibly) and slow variables (underlying conditions that change gradually but may ultimately prove more consequential). This temporal intelligence helps prevent the common trap of sacrificing long-term resilience for short-term stability.

Systems literacy involves recognizing interconnections, feedback loops, and leverage points within complex environments. It requires mapping how interventions in one area might trigger cascading effects elsewhere, identifying potential tipping points where small changes could produce outsized results, and locating places where modest investments might yield disproportionate gains in adaptive capacity. This system's perspective helps prevent the common error of optimizing components at the expense of whole-system resilience.

Implementation literacy focuses on the practical skills needed to execute adaptive changes. This includes knowing when to use incremental approaches versus transformative ones, how to sequence changes to build momentum, and how to sustain energy through extended adaptation processes. It also involves developing "tactical patience," the ability to allow solutions to emerge rather than forcing predetermined outcomes.

Developing resilience literacy requires dedicated learning practices. These include scenario planning exercises that explore multiple possible futures; after-action reviews that extract lessons from successes and failures alike; cross-boundary exchanges that expose organizations to different adaptive approaches; and regular assessment of adaptive capacity using resilience indicators. Through these practices, individuals and organizations develop contextual intelligence about when to persist and when to pivot, continuously refactoring their approaches to align with emerging realities.

By approaching resilience as an ongoing process of learning and adaptation rather than a fixed destination, we develop the capacity not just to survive disruption but to harness it as a catalyst for growth. The continuous refactoring of our systems, strategies, and mindsets becomes not just a response to change but a proactive practice that anticipates and shapes it, creating the conditions for sustained thriving in an inherently uncertain world.

As we reach the end of our journey through system resilience, it's worth reflecting on the fundamental truth that has guided our exploration: pressure and change are not just inevitable; they are essential catalysts for growth. The systems we've examined, whether technological architectures, organizational structures, or personal frameworks, all share a common pattern. Those that survive and thrive are not necessarily the strongest or the most elegantly designed at the outset, but rather those most adaptable to change when pressure mounts.

In our increasingly interconnected world, where complexity grows exponentially and failure points can cascade with startling speed, the practice of continuous refactoring has emerged as perhaps our most valuable discipline. The organizations that have internalized this principle don't wait for systems to break before evolving them. Instead, they cultivate what we might call "anticipatory resilience," the capacity to sense strain before it becomes structural damage.

Consider how our case studies consistently revealed that resilience is rarely achieved through a single heroic intervention. Rather, it emerges through countless small, intentional refactoring's, each representing a hypothesis about how the system might better withstand future pressures. The most resilient teams we encountered documented not just their successes but their near misses, creating rich databases of organizational memory that informed future refactoring efforts. As you apply these principles within your own systems, remember that resilience is not an end state but a dynamic equilibrium. The work of strengthening systems is never complete because the environment itself is constantly evolving. What worked yesterday may not be tomorrow. This is not cause for despair but for humility and curiosity. Perhaps the most powerful insight to take forward is that resilience thrives at the intersection of structure and adaptability. Too much rigidity creates brittleness; too much flexibility leads to chaos. The art lies in creating systems with strong enough foundations to withstand pressure, yet modular and loosely coupled enough to evolve when needed.

In closing, I hope this book has provided not just practical techniques for refactoring systems under pressure, but a fundamental shift in perspective about how we design for an uncertain future. The most resilient systems aren't those that never break; they're those designed to break in small, recoverable ways, continuously learning and evolving in response.

The path toward resilience begins with accepting vulnerability, continues through mindful refactoring, and never truly ends. In embracing this journey, we don't just build stronger systems; we become more resilient ourselves.